The Mountain Artisans Quilting Book

THE MOUNTAIN ARTISANS QUILTING BOOK

Alfred Allan Lewis

Macmillan Publishing Co., Inc.
NEW YORK

Collier Macmillan Publishers
LONDON

Macmillan Publishing Co., Inc.
866 Third Avenue, New York, N.Y. 10022
Collier-Macmillan Canada Ltd.
Library of Congress Catalog Card Number: 72-91259
Fourth Printing 1974
Printed in the United States of America
Photographs by Tom Hodges

CONTENTS

Chapter Five   *18*

Chapter Six   *115*

Chapter Seven   *153*

Index   *179*

INTRODUCTION

In the last few years, Americans have been searching their collective past for the old values and traditions that made this country the greatest experiment in democracy that the world has ever known. There have been revivals of the populist movement in politics and communes in both rural and urban life. We have witnessed great crusades to retrieve rivers and lakes from the ravages of industrial pollution, our countryside from the defoliation of strip mining, our foods from poisonous chemicals.

A renewed interest in ancient handicrafts has been a part of this tremendous effort to return to fundamentals. Even in big cities, people are suddenly wanting to do for themselves. They want the satisfaction that emanates from enjoying the products of their own labors.

For instructions in the old crafts, they have sought out the people of those areas where the traditional skills still flourish as part of the way of life. Appalachia is one of those regions.

In the hollows of the West Virginia mountains, the men still practice their considerable skills in woodworking, pottery making, and glass blowing. The women still possess an enviable facility for weaving, rug hooking, quilting, and all the arts of the needle. As one local matron recently commented, "We live for the day when our girls are old enough to hold a needle."

Out of these hills has come a renaissance in the craft of quilting that has helped to change the look of contemporary fashion and home decoration. The Mountain Artisans is the group that has been most responsible for calling attention to the glories of the old craft. Headquartered in Charleston, the state capital, the Artisans is a non-profit cooperative business, owned and operated by the women who live in the hills and hollows and actually do the quilting.

They have made quilted fabrics that have been used by distinguished interior designers like Parish Hadley, the firm that assisted

Mrs. John F. Kennedy in redoing the White House, as well as such well-known dress designers as Oscar de la Renta and Donald Brooks. Their own unique creations—in quilts and frocks—can be found in fashionable stores across the country, ranging from Saks Fifth Avenue to Neiman Marcus.

The national quilting craze has led to attic and countryside hunts for antique covers. The examples unearthed have been of such phenomenal merit that they've inspired shows at art galleries both here and abroad. The 1971 quilting exhibition at the Whitney Museum, in New York City, was so spectacularly successful that requests for repeat performances came from all over the world.

It was only natural that many women should want to try their hand at this craft that was so much a part of the lives of their grandmothers. No other craft results in things that are as practical as they are beautiful. Not only does a quilt decorate a home, but it offers protection against the inclement weather. Quilted skirts and dresses last for years and are so timeless in design that they never seem to go out of style.

Not only is quilting a rewarding way to spend leisure time, but it is easy to learn. There are only three basic steps to be mastered, and each of these steps can be employed alone or linked in endless variety with the others.

Although quilting is the generic term for the entire craft, it is only one step and can be used independently to festoon a cover or skirt of a solid fabric. The second basic step is piecing. That, too, can be used alone to make things like placemats, pillows, or skirts. The third step is appliqué, and what is true of piecing is also true of it. Of course, the most exciting thing is to use the three together, as in the Dresden Plate skirt (see fig. 50 page 100).

With the instructions from the expert Mountain Artisans, it will become very clear that quilting is quite simple to master. The teaching in this book will be done by women who have grown up in the tradition, having learned the craft from their mothers and grandmothers and greatgrandmothers in an unbroken family chain of quilting that extends back over hundreds of years.

There are some moderns who have resisted the basic appeal of the craft, because they've felt that it could not fit into their jet-speed life-styles. Tourism and travel have become a great industry. People are on the move. People want hobbies that go on trips with them— things like crewel and needlepoint that can be done on beaches or in planes, trains, and buses.

These explorers of faraway places feel that quilting isn't for them, because it isn't portable. They could not be more wrong! Once the preliminary cutting is done, there is absolutely no reason why the materials for piecing or appliqué cannot be carried around in a little bag and stitched together by hand anywhere that the quilter happens to be.

Quilting has certain advantages over different forms of needle-work. For one thing, it's far less expensive than most. There is no need to go to an expensive shop for supplies and instructions. Once the basics are mastered, the crafter can duplicate any quilted item simply by studying it. The materials can be cut from old clothes, sheets, and slipcovers that had been intended for no better use than dust rags. At worst, materials can be purchased for the most nominal sums at remnants and fabric outlet shops. The most extravagant piece of equipment is a sewing machine, which most women probably already own. And even that is not absolutely necessary. After all, our ancestors did some remarkable work without them.

Another virtue of quilting is that, once the last stitch is completed, the work is finished. There is no additional cost and wait while it is sent out to be blocked or made into a pillow, cover, or rug.

Quilting can also be a very sociable hobby. As the ladies of the hollows have been doing for generations, the new quilters can visit and gossip and exchange views as they gather round a quilting frame and do the stitching (see Plate I facing page 6).

What more can any hobbyist want? Here is a craft that is at once inexpensive, productive of immediate results, self-contained, portable, solitary, and social.

All that remains is to learn how—the Mountain Artisans' way —and that's one of the things this book is about. The other is the telling of the inspiring story of a group of gallant and industrious women who banded together to help themselves by using the skills they had been practicing since childhood. In the process, they happened to start a small revolution in fashion that resulted in winning the industry's most coveted honor, the Coty Award.

Diamond Tufted quilt.

CHAPTER ONE

"This quilt's a piece of livin' history. It speaks to me in voices long passed away."

—An Upsher County, West Virginia, quilter

BEFORE learning how to quilt, one should realize that it is more than a "loving hands at home" craft. It is a proud and venerable skill so ancient that nobody knows exactly where or how it began. They only know why. First, there was the necessity for warmth. This was very quickly married to an innate craving for beauty. From this union there issued an artisan craft that, at its best, is an art form.

Some historians claim that civilization started in the Tigris-Euphrates valley, others say it all began along the Nile, and still others make a good case for the banks of the Ganges. In a search for the first quilters, it makes no difference which of these areas one champions. Remnants of quilted fabric have come down to us from the earliest settlements along each of the rivers. In a fanciful mood, one might say that the cradle of civilization was made up with a quilted cover.

The early quilts were indeed rudimentary, no more than a layer of flax or wool sandwiched between two layers of woven fabric and stitched together. Their purposes were purely practical. Even in tropical and subtropical climates, the nights often brought a chill dampness off the waters.

Time and the need for creative expression brought a sophistication to all of the crafts. The men found creative outlets in building, metalwork, and pottery. For the women, there was the loom and the needle.

None of these valleys was a place possessed of any special scenic loveliness—a certain grandeur, but none of the more gentle facets of beauty. The desire for it was as painfully felt as the hunger and thirst during the parched, dry seasons. The women did what they could to soften their surroundings, to make them pretty. The fabrics were dyed brilliant colors and etched with fine embroidery or encrusted with stones. The patterns for quilting became intricate, the stitches delineating designs of extreme complexity and decorativeness.

It took over two thousand years for quilting to reach Europe from the East. In the Middle Ages, the crusading knights marched off in search of God and returned with plunder from an Asiatic civilization. The baggage caravans were filled with jewels, rich cloths, the seeds for exotic vegetation, and so many relics of the true cross that one would have thought Christ had been crucified many times over. Beneath their heavy armor they wore quilted undergarments to shield them from the rigors of the desert elements. Their ladies had never seen anything comparable to the tripart fabrics and, at first, considered them only Oriental oddities. It took a great calamity to awaken them to the practical nature of quilting.

The harshest winter in the history of Europe was visited upon the continent in the fourteenth century. It came again the next year and the year after that. For the first time in anybody's memory, the big rivers froze, landlocking London, Paris, and Hamburg. The women looked again at the quilted cloths but with a new curiosity, one inspired by necessity rather than novelty.

The first European quilts were rather primitive creations held together by a few strong anchor stitches and resembling the pallets upon which most people slept. The word itself came from the Old French *cuilte*, meaning mattress. These original covers were neither handsome nor very durable. The sturdiness and looks of the quilts could have been improved by more numerous, evenly distributed smaller stitches. But the quilts were so cumbersome to handle that additional needlework would have been an onerous chore.

A solution evolved very shortly. Fine embroidery was already a commonplace among the women of medieval Europe. The embroidery frame had been invented and was in wide use among the gentry. The quilting problem disappeared when someone had the idea of expanding and modifying this gadget, so that it could hold a quilt. With time and work it was transformed into what we know as the quilting frame. (See fig. 1 page 3.)

At first, the stitching was in simple straight vertical, horizontal, or diagonal lines (see fig. 2 page 4), but a need for a more decora-

A

Fig. 1. *The quilting frame.*
   A. The horses and side strips that are assembled into a quilting frame.
   B. Detail of one of the notches that are at both ends of the horse.
   C. Fitting the side strip into the notches.

B

C

D. *The assembled quilting frame.*

FIG. 2. *Early quilting patterns (the broken lines represent the stitches).*

4

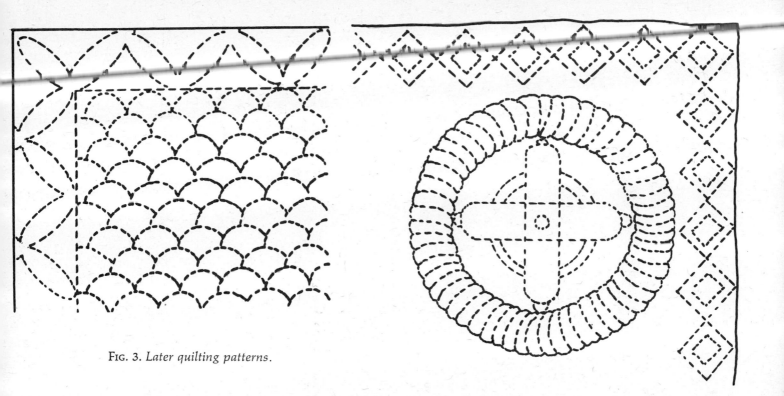

Fig. 3. *Later quilting patterns.*

tive and artistic expression again surfaced among the craftswomen. (See fig. 3 page 5.) Quilting evolved into a form of running-stitch embroidery in which the needle pierced all three layers of the cover, linking them and holding them firmly in place. It was not long before all sorts of ornamental embroidery patterns found their way into quilting: floral arrangements, coats of arms, scrolls, and beribboned garlands began to be depicted in fine stitchery. A light sketch of the desired design was made on the top of the coverlet; then the needle and thread followed its lines. For the drawings, the ladies used a soluble drawing material that would disappear in laundering.

As the needlework grew more complex and decorative, experiments were made using finer fabrics than the original homespuns. Silks and cottons, linens and satins, velvets and brocades became the fashionable materials among the nobility. Finally, with their heightened beauty, quilted fabrics were adapted for use in the making of clothing of unparalleled richness.

Each region of Europe made its own contribution to a craft that was already starting to take on the proportions of an art form. The basic techniques grew, as methods from other crafts were adapted to it.

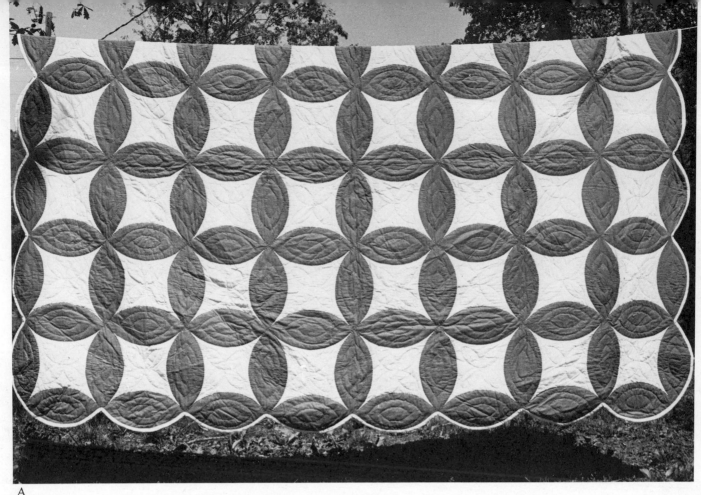

A

FIG. 4. *Traditional appliqué quilt.*
    A. Traditional appliqué quilt made to resemble interlocking circles by the careful
      placement of oval appliquéd pieces and the scalloping of the border.
    B. Detail of the quilting pattern. Notice the fine, even stitchery.
    C. Detail of the back of the quilt, showing the stitches going all the way through
      batting and backing to form as fine a design on the reverse side.

B   C

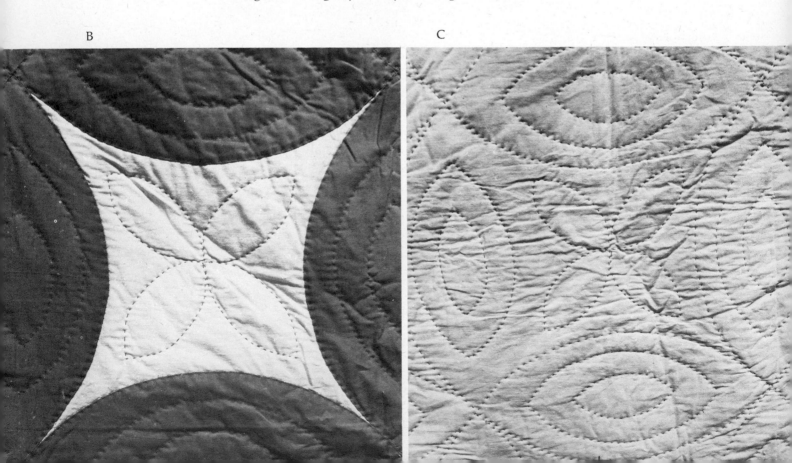

PLATE I. *Women at Sod, gathered around a quilting frame.*

PLATE II. *Old and new Crazy quilt hanging on a clothesline.*

PLATE III. *Modern adaptation of traditional Crazy quilt.*

PLATE IV. *Florette Angel's bedroom with an assortment of Mountain Artisan pillows, including Grab the Crab.*

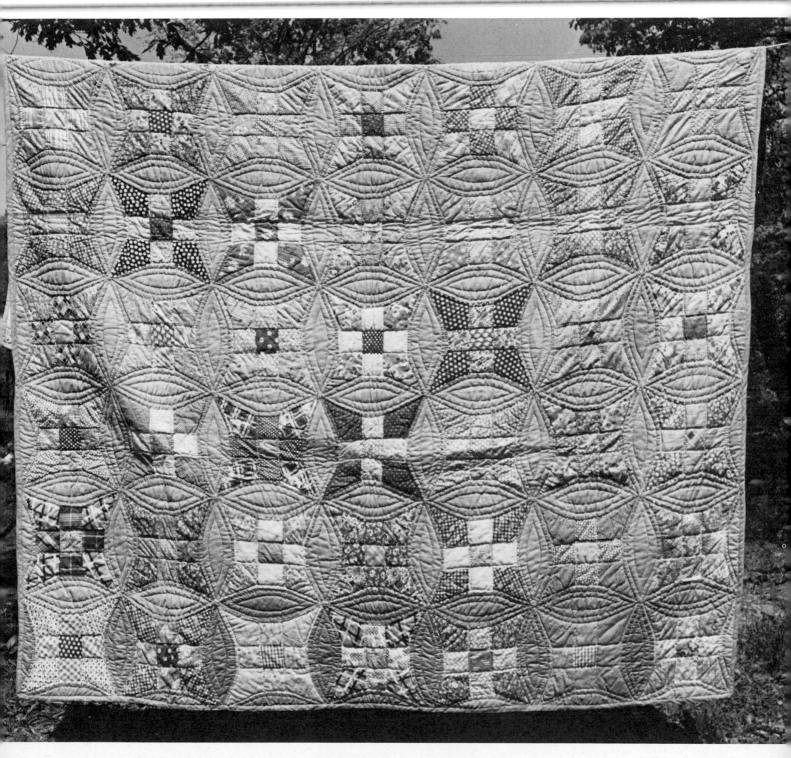

FIG. 5. *Variation on the circular appliquéd quilt with patchwork inset.*

French culture has always been one of decorative distillation. Its architecture, cuisine, and couture are intricate refinements of the Flemish and Italian styles. The ladies of France added a new dimension to the already popular quilted floral patterns by cutting botanical shapes out of contrasting materials, appliquéing them to the cover layer of the quilt, and then doing the actual quilting in outline around the appliqué. (See fig. 6 page 8.)

After casting out the Moors in the fifteenth century, Spain became the most Catholic nation in Europe, and its quilters were the first to use their craft in ecclesiastical vestments.

The best Italian quilting was done in the Kingdom of the Two Sicilies. Because of the sultry climate, quilted material was largely used ornamentally rather than for warmth. The most popular fabric was a delicate, handloomed linen, and the favorite stitch was one of their own invention, the *trapunto* (or Italian cable stitch). To execute it, cording is inserted beneath the top layer of the coverlet or fabric, and the stitching done around the cording so that it serves to raise or pad the often intricate quilting design. (See fig. 7 page 9.)

Because of the cold and damp winters, quilts were an absolute necessity in Flanders and the British Isles. So great were the demands for the covers that a primitive version of a cottage industry grew up. The peasant women made rough, homely quilts for themselves and fine, delicate ones for their feudal lords.

FIG. 6. *French appliqué and quilting pattern.*

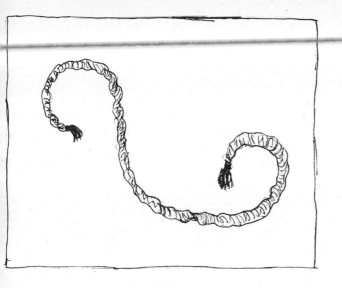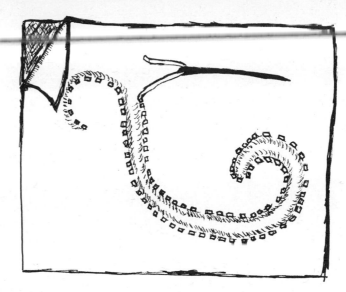

Fig. 7. Trapunto.

As the quilter's mastery of her craft increased, a coverlet began to be judged by both the number of stitches in it and the artfulness of their arrangement and execution. The rivalry in "compleat stitcherie" grew keener, and the areas between the two dominant design clusters—elaborate central pattern and intricately worked borders—also had to be filled. The filling stitchery was generally determined by the shape of the central pattern; if it was round or curved, the linking quilting was in crossing straight lines that defined geometric shapes such as squares, rectangles, diamonds, or parallelograms. If the central pattern was geometric, the fill inscribed circles, shells, waves, or arches. (See fig. 8 page 10.)

It was not only the common people who could count the years of their lives in the threads of a quilt. Queen Mary of Scotland was imprisoned for twenty years by her cousin, Queen Elizabeth of England. Those monotonous years, with their brief moments of hope and long months of despair, can be ticked off in the many examples of her exquisite needlepoint and quilting that are exhibited to this day in Hardwicke Hall, her royal jail.

The European craft of quilting began to lose its creative vitality toward the end of the sixteenth century. But western quilting did not die. It surged forward and found new inspiration in the American colonies. Quilts were an essential part of the household goods

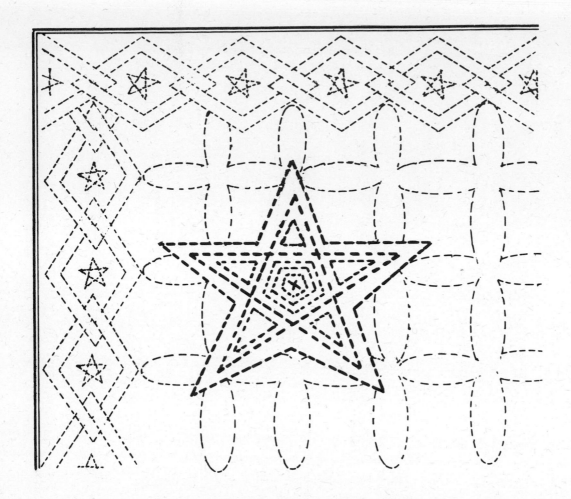

FIG. 8. *British quilting pattern (curved stitchery to link geometric design).*

that the early colonists brought along on their journey to the New World. They were coming to an alien, mysterious and possibly hostile land. Even the most elementary comforts would be unavailable, and if they were to survive the first winter, protection against the cold was of incalculable importance.

Cut off from the traditions and (more to the point) the materials found in abundance in the Old World, quilting underwent an extraordinary transformation. The use of bold colors and abstract patterns brought a vivid new life to the old craft. (See fig. 9 page 11.)

This primitive abstraction and boldness of outlook was often to occur in the development of American crafts as they diverged from

FIG. 9. *Old Pennsylvania quilting and appliqué pattern.*

the European. Snobbish pedants have tended to dismiss this virility as the result of clumsy and inadequately trained artisans. Can one truly call Paul Revere silver or colonial furniture inferior to the products of European counterparts?

It was true that American design invention was often the result of the unavailability of traditional materials. But it was more than that. There was something inherent in the point of view of the people—a daring outlook, a freedom, a willingness to take liberties with design. After Americans became sophisticated and civilized, even by European standards, this birthright still did not die. In the late nineteenth century it could be found in Tiffany glass; and to this day, in art, it can be seen in "pop" and "op" innovations in painting.

However, the first appearance of an indigenously American design was in quilt making. The Americanization of the quilt was

FIG. 10. *Traditional floral appliqué.*
A. Top of a traditional floral appliquéd spread before quilting.

B. Detail of one of the flowers, showing use of embroidery for detail and the appliquéd stitchery.

originally the result of the life struggle during the early years on this continent. There were no fabrics except those that the settlers brought with them from the old country. It was years before there was sufficient flax grown or wool produced to provide the raw materials for spinning. As the quilts that were brought from Europe began to wear out, they had to be repaired with bits of fabric from old clothes or from other quilts that were beyond mending. The results were the original patchwork quilts.

As the families moved westward, the quilting tradition went with them. Fabric was still at a premium, and the patchwork quilt remained the prevalent type. Even after the traders started to find their way to the frontier settlements, the patchwork quilt remained in favor. Hardship and poverty were certainly the contributing motivation for this. It was a saving to patch rather than discard.

But there was something more. Winters were long and bleak. Color fled from the landscape. Crude log cabins were drab and cheer-. less reminders of a poverty the people did not really feel. Where there was so much freedom and promise, there could be no deep conviction that the overwhelming burden of poverty was a permanent condition of life. Things would get better. They knew it in their hearts and sang it in their psalms.

The women hungered for color and gaiety, for something decorative as well as useful, and they found those qualities in their quilts. As the patches began to dominate the quilts, something wonderful was happening. New and fantastic shapes were forming. It was not long before quilts were being made by stitching the patches together without any background fabric. Odd bits of material were sewn in strange and fanciful juxtaposition to each other. The only coordination of design was the selective and instinctive good taste of the crafters. The crazy quilt had been invented. (See fig. 11 page 14.)

There was also the yearning for tradition and roots. This, too, found its way into quilting. That bit of silk was from the gown

FIG. 11. *Crazy quilt.*

Grandma brought from England. That flannel was the shirt Papa bought before starting out from Philadelphia. That calico print was the baby's dress. The history of life—the hardships, the happiness, the tragedy—were all there in the quilts—the threads and fabric of a family chronicle.

The quest for companionship, gossip, and the homely things that softened the struggle for survival ended in the quilting parties that illumined the long, gray winter days. The three layers of cover, stuffing, and backing were put into the frame (see fig. 14 page 19), and the women gathered around it to quilt together and do for each other. When Emma Jackson's coverlet was finished, they started on one for Rebecca Collins, and so it went, until each woman in the group had a new cover, and the cycle began anew.

Practical needs were satisfied simply by making the quilts, but the creative and decorative impulses sought deeper fulfillment. In addition to the quilting stitch, innumerable embroidery stitches began to make their appearance. As an artist feels a need to sign his work, so the ladies began to embroider their names on their creations. Some crazy quilts had as many embroidered signatures as they had individual pieces of fabric, and these were called friendship quilts. They commemorated a given time and place, when the women gathered in comraderie. They remained as loving mementoes long after the families had moved on in the ever-westward flow.

Quilts were often the only gifts the women could afford to give. They served as community presents to new brides and mothers and as tokens of sympathy to families whose homes and possessions were destroyed by the frequent fires in those settlements of rough log cabins lit by candle and warmed by open hearth.

Early crazy and patchwork quilts depended upon the color and variety of sizable pieces of fabric. No matter how broad the range of materials, there tended to be a predictability about the results.

There was also a practical consideration that inspired fresh inventiveness. Because of the nature of the qulits the women were making, small pieces of material were often discarded. Good cloth was expensive and still far from easy to obtain. The waste offended these economical ladies. Out of the small remnants they began to piece larger blocks that, in turn, were sewn together to make the quilts.

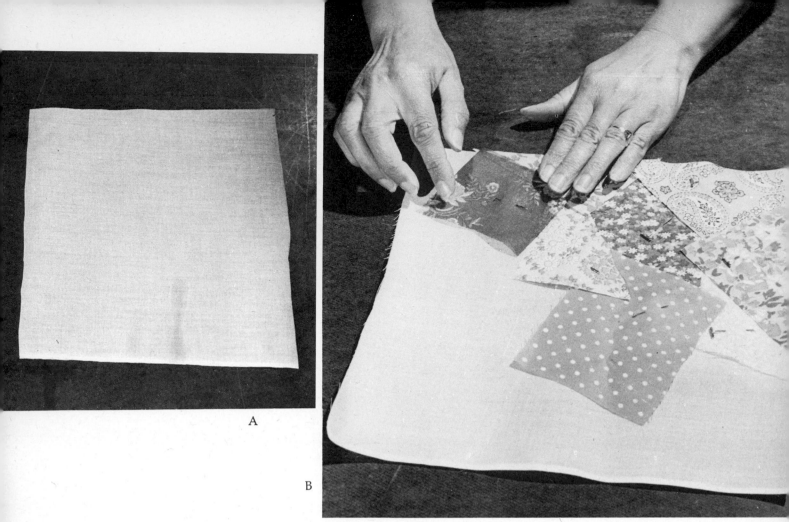

A

B

FIG. 12. *Making a block for a Crazy quilt.*

    A. A block for a Crazy quilt can be made with a fabric backing. Cut a piece of fabric to the desired size of the block.

    B. Cut or gather small odd-shaped pieces of fabric. They can be different in each block or repeat in each block. Pin them to the block. As they are pinned, overlap the pieces randomly.

    C. After covering the block with the random pieces of fabric, prepare to sew them in place by folding under an edge.

C

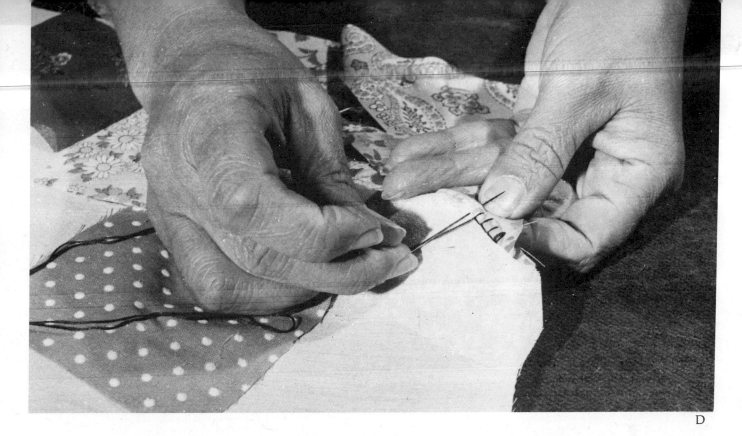

D

D. For this particular block, a buttonhole stitch is used (see pages 174–175) to attach the pieces to the backing. A zigzag would also have served and could have been done on a machine.

E. The completed Crazy quilt block.

F. A view of the back, showing how the stitchery outlines the pieces in the block.

E

F

A

FIG. 13. *Crazy quilt.*

    A. Traditional Crazy quilt. Notice the great variations in the blocks.

    *B. Detail of tufting on the Crazy quilt. Many strands of multicolored wool were
      tied together to give a fullness to the tufts.*

B

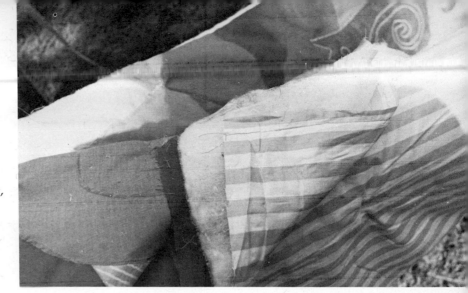

FIG. 14. *The three layers of a quilt assembled for quilting: the backing, batting, and cover.*

The piecing gradually became refined and started to take on a decorative individuality. The pieces were cut to uniform size so that the blocks could repeat each other. When they were linked to form the quilt top, they took on still another design. (See fig. 15 page 19.) That uniquely American contribution to quilting, the pieced quilt, had been born.

The designs became fanciful and humorous abstractions of the flowers of a region and of the commonplaces and superstitions of life on the frontier. Often, the same design would crop up in two different areas and receive a different name in each one.

FIG. 15. *Tree of Life. To construct Tree of Life, you need forty small triangles the same color as the block, forty of the same size in a shade of green or a green print. For the trunk, you need a large rectangle, a large triangular top, and a large trapezoid base. Attach these parts to form the pieced tree, and then appliqué it to the background block.*

FIG. 16. *Old Maid's Puzzle. A completely pieced block made of thirty-two triangles (see Slashed Diagonal page 60)—eighteen of the dominant color, eight of the next strongest color, and six of the least dominant color.*

15

16
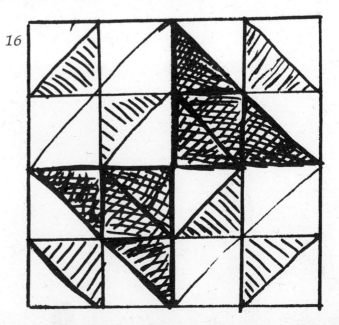

The names were often as evocative as the covers. The Tree of Life, the Rose of Sharon, Drunkard's Path, Robbing Peter to Pay Paul, Flying Geese, Crown and Cross, World without End, Palm Leaf, Dresden Plate, Old Maid's Puzzle. (See fig. 16 page 19.) Many of these were a combination of appliqué and piecing. The central design motif was pieced together and then appliquéd on a solid block. The blocks were then linked to form the quilt.

Quilting reached its zenith in America toward the end of the eighteenth century. The industrial revolution of the next century marked its decline. By the 1880s, cheap and attractive machine-made covers were readily available, although none could approach the artistry and beauty of the handmade quilt. The tradition of quilting began to disappear except in rural areas. With it went many of the handcrafts that so enriched the lives of our ancestors and that were, through human inventiveness, so often raised to the level of art forms.

For nearly one hundred years, the art of quilt making lingered only in places overlooked by the often overrated glories of progress. It is from these regions that the skill has returned once again to enrich the American cultural heritage.

CHAPTER TWO

"That quilt's a part of the family. It's come down from eldest daughter to eldest daughter since—oh, I couldn't rightly say when. Long before the War between the States."

—Lewis County quilter

In the early days of the Republic, there was a custom of embroidering in its border the year in which a cover was finished. The oldest dated quilt in America is now in Dumbarton House, in Washington, D.C. The date is 1795. It also bears the initials of the quilter, W.T.G., and it was made in what is now West Virginia. Along with these fine old heirloom quilts, the skills and secrets of their construction have been preserved in mountain families.

In the hollows of the Appalachian Mountains, the tradition of native crafting has thrived uninterruptedly for over two hundred years. It is a part of the lives of the people who make their homes in this impressive mountain range that sweeps down from New England to Alabama, forming a natural barrier between the busy commercial Eastern coast and the rich farmlands of the Midwest.

Life in those hills has always been so harsh—and eking out a livelihood so difficult—that the stranger wonders why the early pioneers stopped there instead of persevering to the sweeter lands beyond. Perhaps it was because of an inborn sense of beauty, for the rugged hills are also poetically beautiful—dappled with the colors of a crazy quilt in the warm seasons, burnished with orange flame in the autumn, sparkling with pristine snow in the winter.

The people seemed to have been molded by this environment, at once as rugged and as beautiful as the land in which they dwell. Even in the difficult circumstances forced upon them by an unyielding terrain, they remain proud and independent. The old ways and beliefs do not die easily; a sense of family runs deep within them, and a collective memory traces its way back to the very beginning of this country. They work not merely to survive, but because this is fundamentally what it means to be human. Work gives them dignity within the family and among neighbors. Charity is anathema, except in the form of the help they give to one another out of a common familial sense.

They do for themselves, making with their own hands what cannot be bought in the stores. The secrets of the old crafts—quilting, preserving, and making furniture, glass, pottery, soap, medicines, and even moonshine whiskey—have been passed down through the generations and have prospered despite encroaching industrialization.

And among the rest of us who do not live in the hills, a sense of loss, a longing for something torn away in the process of becoming a mechanized nation, an anger at the environment-poisoning byproducts of this atomic age, have engendered a need to make a personal statement by means of the old crafts.

For those who wish to learn how to quilt, there are no better teachers than the women of West Virginia. These splendid women cannot remember a time when quilting was not a part of their lives. Their pleasure in their work is something wonderful to behold.

Mrs. Blanche Griffith, of Sod, a small community some fifty miles from Charleston, has been quilting all of her life. An extremely articulate woman, she has given lovely expression to her feelings about the craft.

"The gift for quilting is like the gift for music. You have to love it. It's *borned* in you. You have to want to create beautiful things. If you've got it—well, you just naturally make things that are beautiful. If you turn them out any old way, you can see it by just looking at them. Can't you tell the difference between these homemade quilts and the machine-made ones? In the ones done by hand, you can see the love, and the thought, and the care.

"When the old ones was pieced, probably, the mother was thinking, I'll give it to one of my children as a wedding present. It'll be handed down through the generations.

PLATE V. *Sharon Rockefeller wearing one of the first pieced skirts ever made by the Mountain Artisans.*

PLATE VI. *Fence Rail quilt.*

PLATE VII. *Roman Stripe quilt*.

PLATE VIII. *Log Cabin quilt (variation by color grouping)*.

"My daughter's sewed all her life—just like I've done. When I started with my mother, we had a quilting frame at home, and we all gathered around it. I stood up before I was old enough to sit on a chair. When mother would be quilting, she'd thread a needle, and she'd give it to us, and we'd sew pieces together and make doll's clothes and things like that.

"Mothers used to give children things to do to keep them out of meanness. Nowadays, all they do is get out and get into meanness. Mothers was proud of their daughters when they could sew, and cook, and things like that. If you had a daughter, and she couldn't do, you wouldn't want anybody to know it.

"The ladies around here have been quilting all their lives. And there's an awful lot of young ones, too. People are saying they can't—it's not true. All they need is to want to—to feel that love."

In Mrs. Griffith's family, there are two quilts linking five generations (see Plate II facing page 6). She said,

"The new quilt was made by my daughter. The old one was pieced by my greatgrandmother and given to my mother. And she gave it to me. When I was a child, mother would take the quilt and spread it out. And she'd tell us stories of the pieces. This was Aunt So-and-so's dress. And that was So-and-so's wedding dress. And things like that. So, it was really an entertainment to us. I don't rightly know how old it is. Well over a hundred years. My mother's ninety-two. And her grandmother pieced the quilt and was dead before she was ever born.

"The stitching and embroidery's similar in both. But you can see the difference in the colors. They didn't make such bright colors back then. It was all more practical— clothes and things. They used all kinds of fabrics. See there. Worsteds, and serge, and taffeta—silk and velvet."

A

Fig. 17. Making a Jigsaw placemat.

    A. Select six different patterned fabrics, in color of choice. One-half yard of each will make at least a dozen placemat tops, and a 2½-yard piece of 45-inch fabric will make a dozen placemat backings. Cut the fabrics into sets of strips measuring 2¾" wide, 4¾" wide, and 6¾".

    B. Using cardboard patterns, 2¾" by 5", 4¾" by 5", 6¾" by 5", for measuring, cut up the corresponding strips.

    C. Separate the cut pieces into stacks.

B

C

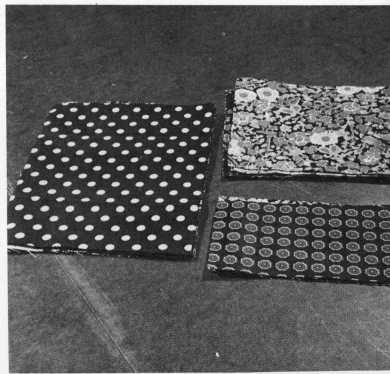

D

D. Using random selection, take pieces of fabric from each stack and lay them out, overlapping the ends ⅜", to a length of 20¾". Two 6¾" pieces, one 4¾", and two 2¾" pieces would produce this. So would one 6¾", two 4¾", and three 2¾" pieces.

E. Stitch together the pieces, using a ⅜" seam allowance, to form one row measuring 20¾" by 5".

F. Make a second row the same length. Use the first row as a guide to make certain that patterns and seams in both rows do not fall together. Attach the first row to the second row, using a ⅜" seam allowance.

E

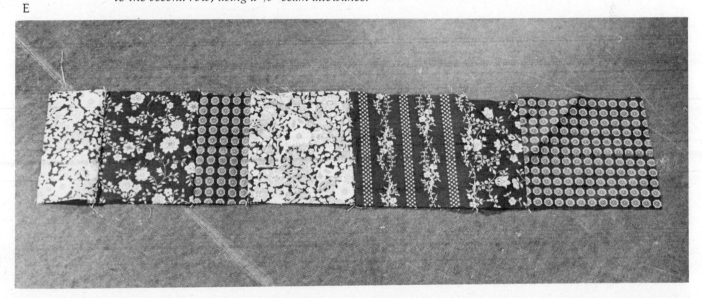

F

G

H

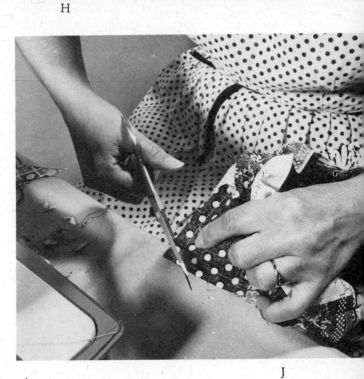

I

J

G. Make a third row and attach it to the other two.

H. Using a piece of cardboard, measuring 13¾" by 20¾", cut a piece of fabric to use as backing for the mat. The pattern is not necessary, if one uses a ruler and pencil and carefully draws a rectangle, measuring 13¾" by 20¾", on the reverse side of the backing fabric and then cuts it out.

I. With the reverse sides of the pieced block and backing facing out, leave a ⅜" seam allowance and stitch them together on 3½ sides.

J. Clip the corners with scissors.

26

K

L

K. *Through the half side opening, pull the placemat right-side out. Using a hidden stitch, stitch up the rest of the mat.*

L. *Using a contrasting cotton, do a running stitch border, ⅜" in, all around the mat.*

M. *The finishing touch of the border.*

N. *The front and rear of finished jigsaw placemats. In the one shown, nine fabrics were used and the size was extended to measure 24" by 13". The original strips were more varied than simply 2¾", 4¾", and 6¾" widths. This was done to indicate that there is no limit to the variations that can be worked on the jigsaw pattern.*

M

N

Both covers are examples of the early American crazy quilt. An examination of figure 18 discloses the fact that crazy quilts are made in blocks. Because the pieces of each block have no definite geometric relationship to each other, it is best to attach them to some sort of backing rather than directly to each other.

Mrs. Griffith recommends paper for the backing material, because it can be torn away as soon as the stitching is completed. This eliminates an extra layer of fabric when it is time to do the actual quilting.

Embroidery stitches are often part of a crazy quilt, and the easiest way to attach the pieces to the paper is using the zig-zag attachment of a sewing machine. They can also be sewn with ribbon binding or, if the desired effect is hidden stitchery, by tucking the pieces under and using a discreet hemming stitch.

As any West Virginia quilter knows, piecing is an essential element of the quilting craft. A pieced block can serve other functions besides forming part of a quilt. Pieced blocks can make marvelous placemats. One of the more attractive modern pieced designs is the Mountain Artisans' Jigsaw placemat. (See fig. 17(N) page 27.)

If you've never pieced before, the Jigsaw placemat is a wonderful way to begin. First of all, it looks sensational on any table. Second of all, complicated as it looks, it could not be easier to make. Simply follow the directions on pages 24 through 27, and a complete set will be finished in a very short time.

Another virtue of the Jigsaw pattern is its versatility. Depending upon the fabrics selected, it can serve for any meal. In pastel seersuckers and cottons, it's beautiful on the breakfast table or tray. Bright, cheerful prints that complement your luncheon china make it the perfect setting for the midday meal. For a dinner party, nothing could be more elegant than a Jigsaw placemat in rich brocade, velvet, damask, and silk.

As a matter of fact, once the simple skill of piecing is mastered, any of the traditional pieced patterns can be used to make a placemat or tablecloth. Just keep making blocks until the desired size is attained, make a backing, attach, and that's all there is to it.

Single blocks can also be used to make decorative pillows like one of the ones so lavishly heaped upon the bed in the photograph,

A

B

FIG. 18. *Grab the Crab pillow.*

    A. *The crab pattern. To make it, take a 20" square piece of cardboard, heavy paper, or oak tag. In the center, use a compass to inscribe a circle measuring 10" in diameter. Compasses are available in any store that sells school supplies. They cost about twenty-five cents. Set the compass at "5" to make a 10" circle. With a ruler, draw the jointed claws almost to the edge of the square. Then cut.*

    B. *Trace the pattern on the fabric desired for the crab body.*

    C. *Cut out the fabric crab.*

    D. *Pin the crab body to the center of a 20¾" square of the fabric desired for the background.*

C

D

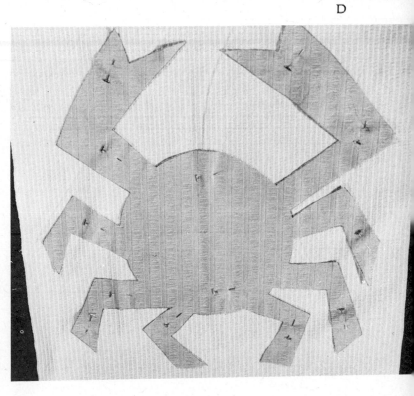

E   F

E. *Lightly sketch the simple details of the crab body and eyes. Using a zigzag stitch, pick them out in a contrasting color of thread. Using the same zigzag stitch and the same thread, appliqué the crab to the square. When zigzag-stitching, a seam allowance is not necessary. Stitch three sides of the back and front of the outer pillow together, following the same instructions given for the inner pillow. Stuff the inner pillow in through the open half side and slip stitch closed or, if you would like to remove the case for laundering, insert a zipper.*

F. *The completed Grab the Crab pillow. If the cording edging is desired, get 2⅓ yards of covered cording in a color complementary to the body of the crab or cover your own. Cording to be covered is available at most piece goods stores selling upholstery fabric. Sew it around the pillow front before connecting front to back to make the completed cover.*

Plate IV, facing p. 7. Close scrutiny will disclose one that is an absolute joy to make. Propped up in the front on the left is the unmistakable Grab the Crab pillow.

For the new quilter, who has never tried appliqué, the second important basic of quilting, Grab the Crab makes a droll start. For a 20″-square pillow, cut two 20¾″ squares from any fabric you select. A solid color is preferable but not essential. If a print is used, it's best to cut the crab from a complementary solid fabric. The reverse is true when a print crab is selected.

An inner pillow is suggested but not essential. To make it, cut two 20¾″ squares from some inexpensive unbleached cotton or muslin. The extra ¾″ is to allow a ⅜″ seam allowance on all sides.

Stitch the inner pillow closed, leaving approximately five inches open on one side. Snip a small triangle, outside the stitches, from each of the corners. Turn the inner pillow right-side out through the opening and fill with dacron stuffing. Slip-stitch the rest of the inner pillow closed and put it aside until the outer pillow is completed. Now follow the instructions in figure 18 (A-F).

Hard times and home crafts—those were two things that the people of the West Virginia hills knew very well. During the 1930s, when the entire nation was going through the worst financial crisis in its history, a plan was formulated that would utilize the crafts to alleviate the poverty of the Appalachian area.

Eleanor Roosevelt spearheaded a project to train a sufficient number of local craftsmen to start small community industries throughout the region. Under the Works Projects Administration (WPA), arts and crafts centers were started for the development of skills along lines that would eventually produce marketable commodities.

Quilters, weavers, caners, carpenters, and glass blowers were among the categories represented. After the training period, the workers were gathered into independent cottage industries. But there was one point that had been overlooked in all of the scrupulous planning by the WPA. Nobody had given any thought to marketing the products so that they could become available to potential customers. For the idealists in charge of the project, the creation of employment was all that mattered. Its perpetuation through sales was not their problem.

The start of World War II signaled the end of the program. The government became involved in the more pressing need of the production of strategic materials. The local crafts movement was pigeon-holed and finally abondoned. The impressive stone buildings that housed the crafts centers still stand, but their purpose is forgotten. They serve as garages, inns, and restaurants.

The project had died without even approaching the fulfillment of its noble aims. But the skills continued to develop, the talents uncovered did not die off. The craftsmen were often exploited by dealers who came into Appalachia and bought the quilts and other fine handmade products for such ludicrously low sums that they did not even bring the price of their labors up to the guaranteed national minimum wage. These same goods were later resold as luxury items, bringing high profits to the exploiters.

In the postwar period there was much talk about Appalachian poverty. Many articles that were written humiliated the proud people of the hills and hollows by underscoring only the negative part of their condition. A journalistic xenophobia developed in the area. Nobody wrote of the humor and courage of the mountaineers, of their skills that were as finely honed as those of an artist. Everybody was willing to do a lot of talking about their dilemma, but nobody was doing anything to help them to help themselves. They did not want hand-outs—they were not that breed—they wanted to do for themselves, and they could, if only somebody would open the door and point the direction. It was not until a great tragedy brought a country boy, not unlike themselves, to the White House that anything was actually done for them.

A lot has been said, pro and con, about the presidency of Lyndon Baines Johnson, but his war on poverty at home should not be forgotten, nor can it be too highly praised.

The establishment of the Office of Economic Opportunity, in 1964, opened the door a little for artisans like the quilters. Through that narrow passage there entered a very determined young woman named Florette Angel.

Looking up from her quilting frame, Mrs. Griffith commented, "If ever anybody was aptly named, it was that girl."

CHAPTER THREE

"When the first settlers came into the hollows, they were poor. It was a hard life in a rugged terrain and climate. Here, the quilting was born of necessity."

—LIBRARIAN, CHARLESTON PUBLIC LIBRARY

I F EVER a state was ready to fight a war on poverty, it was West Virginia. The people had learned long ago that they would have to do without many of the comforts that the rest of the country took for granted. In some counties, the entire landscape had been devastated by destructive strip mining. In others, there was no form of public transportation. In still others, there was neither industry nor adequate farming lands. Unemployment was three times the national average, and the median annual income was less than $3,000.

During the 1950s and 1960s, the state experienced a severe economic depression owing to the collapse of coal mining as a major source of employment. Many of the hill families were on welfare, the men out of work and the women running the homes on little better than nonexistent resources.

These people had skills, motivation, and pride. They hated charity even if it came from the government in the form of unemployment benefits. A plan was needed that would profitably utilize the crafts that had been located and developed during the Works Projects Administration.

The Department of Commerce entered the battle. In the beginning, it made as many mistakes as did the Department of Defense in waging the more belligerent forms of war. Projects were instituted that had immediate results as their only goals. Unfortunately, indiscriminate help does not work like Nescafé. A spoonful of it mixed in the hot water of hard-core poverty does not produce an instant result.

An army of idealistic young people descended upon West Virginia. Some worked as part of a regional group called the Appalachian Volunteers. The vast majority came as part of VISTA (Volunteers In Service To America), the domestic equivalent of the Peace Corps. They worked in coordination with local Community Action programs that were funded by the Office of Economic Opportunity.

In many areas, the newcomers proved enormously effective. Tremendous efforts were made to help the low-income groups to organize themselves. They started voter registration campaigns, fought for a larger local voice on school boards, helped to institute education programs for the young and senior citizen projects for the elderly and, generally, pointed out the long overlooked rights that the poor shared equally with the affluent in the eyes of the law.

In all of these endeavors, they proved extremely valuable to the Community Action people by providing the manpower to carry through programs these local organizations had always felt were necessary. They soon developed deep ties of mutual understanding, affection, and respect with the natives. So profound were these feelings that many felt as if they had truly found a home and remained in the area long after their duties with VISTA were over.

For all their dedication and good intentions, however, there were failures. One notable failure was basically a repetition of what had happened in the 30s. Like those in the Eleanor Roosevelt project, the newcomers could recognize the intrinsic worth of handcrafts. They could even start training programs in the development of them. What they did not know and, given their backgrounds, could not be expected to know was whether or not the products were marketable, how to price them, and how to merchandise them.

In their enthusiasm and great desire to create immediate new sources of income, they wanted dramatic achievement and overnight change. This led to some misunderstanding with local crafters who only wanted some indication that they were not going to be exploited as they had been so often in the past. The mountaineers had lived for generations in the hollows amid their own kind. They would rather do the things they always had done in the manner in which they'd always done them. They were proud of the fact that they could do for themselves. When a new roof was needed, the men would get together and raise it. They had learned how from their fathers and their fathers' fathers before them. These outsiders would have to prove themselves. Promises were cheap. Disappointments were very expensive—they could not afford them.

If the project was a quilt with a simple design like the 81" by 100" Diamond Tufted (see fig. 19 page 35) the quilter could set to work doing it alone. The first thing to do is to prepare a cardboard diamond pattern. It should measure 12" from top point to bottom point and 9" from side point to side point. To construct this, draw a line 12" on the cardboard. Halfway down, cross it with another line 9" wide. Make certain that the lines intersect at their midpoints (6" down for the long line and 4½" across for the shorter line). With a ruler, connect the tips of the cross to form a diamond. Then add ⅜" seam allowance to all four sides, making a larger diamond. (The seam allowance will actually be more than ⅜" at the points.) Cut out this larger diamond (12" by 9" with a ⅜" seam allowance added all around). On a sheet of paper measuring 39" square, trace the diamond as often as it will go. Now follow the directions given in figure 20.

After piecing is completed, place the quilt-top face-down on the floor and cover it with a layer of batting and the backing fabric, face up. One of the fabrics used for the diamonds may be used for backing. Sew the layers together, using a large running stitch, along the edges. Tufting—or, as it is sometimes called, tacking —is used for this spread. Insert the quilt in a quilting hoop and keep going until the quilt is finished. For instructions, see figure 21.

FIG. 19. *Diamond Tufted design and tufting pattern.*

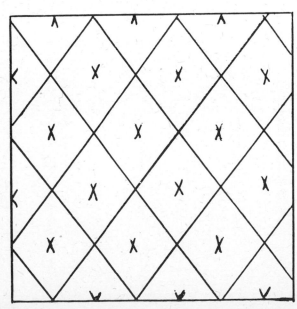

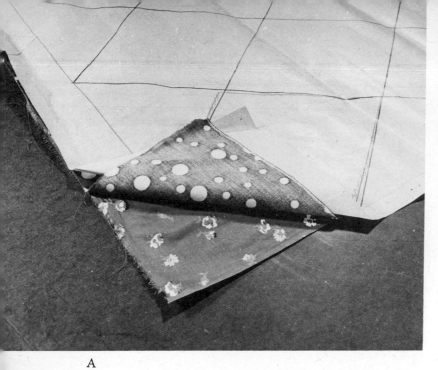

A

B

Fig. 20. *Instructions for Diamond Tufted quilt.*
  A. *On a stack of at least eight different pieces of fabric, measuring 45" by 41", lay the paper with the diamond tracings.*
  B. *Pin the paper to the fabrics and cut along the lines.*
  C. *First, cut long strips.*
  D. *Cut the strips into diamonds.*

C

D

E   F

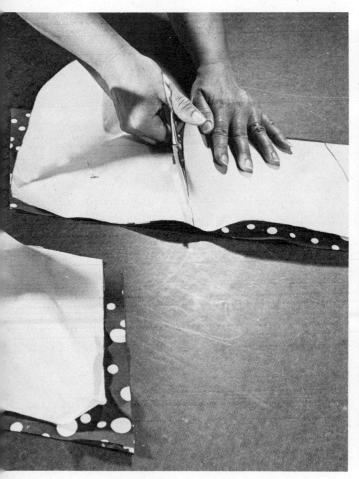 

E. Continue until all the strips are cut. Reserve the half-diamonds at the end of each strip. They will be important for piecing.

F. Piece the quilt in diagonal rows. When there are sufficient rows to make the quilt, piece the rows together. Fill in the jagged ends with the half-diamonds that were saved in the cutting. In piecing the rows, be careful that the seams are lined up to make unbroken diagonal lines. For all piecing use the 3/8" seam allowance.

A

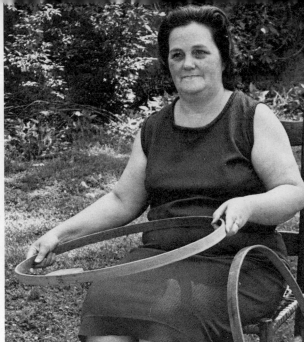

B

FIG. 21. Tufting in quilting hoop.

    A. The quilting hoop. The outer half is on the left, and the inner half is on the right.

    B. The quilter takes up the inner half of the hoop.

    C. She places the quilt to be tufted over the inner half and positions the outer half
       on top of it.

C

D

E

D. *After smoothing the quilt over the inner half, she places the outer half over it*
   and locks it in place by tightening the clamp.
E. *Ready to begin tufting.*
F. *From a ball of wool, cut a small strand.*
G. *Cut several small lengths and put them aside.*

F

G

H

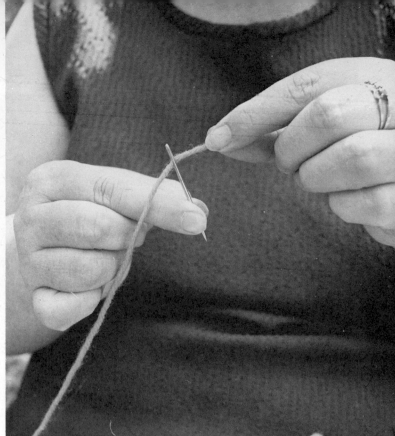

I

H. *Cut a long length of wool.*
I. *Thread it through a needle.*
J. *Catch all the layers of the quilt at the point where the tuft is to be made.*
K. *Pull the wool almost all the way through until only a small tail remains.*

J

K

L

M

L. *After cutting the thread, so that there are two tails, place one of the reserved short pieces in the center.*

M. *Tie the tails over the reserved piece.*

N. *Taking one tail and the reserved piece in the left hand and the other pair in the right hand, tie them together.*

O. *With scissors, even the end, and the tuft is completed.*

N

O

After the last tuft, the quilt is removed from the hoop, bound, and the corners mitered, following the method shown in fig. 22, pages 42–44.

By the way, if the quilter is feeling neighborly, the tufting can be done by inserting the layers in a quilting frame—see fig. 23, page 45—and friends can join in the work. If a frame is not available, stitched quilting can be done in a hoop.

The Giant Maxigon (see fig. 25 page 51) is made in exactly the same fashion, only the pattern is a hexagon, drawn to measure 12″ from top horizontal side to bottom horizontal side, and 12″ from side point to side point. A ⅜″ seam allowance is added on all sides.

The women enjoyed their quilting sessions. It was traditionally a time for socializing as well as enterprising. Gallons of coffee would be consumed, the air thick with cigarette smoke and charged with exchanges of gossip that rendered any local Suzy or Hedda Hopper totally superfluous.

Quilting can be done alone, without either a quilting hoop or frame. After the three layers are securely basted together, start quilting in the middle of the cover and work out to the sides. This can

FIG. 22. *Binding*.
  A. *After the quilting, the last step in completing the cover or spread is binding the edges. For this, commercial seam binding of the desired width and color is used, or make your own to match or complement the quilt material by cutting bias strips of material. Fold out the binding and attach by machine to the top of the quilt.*
  B. *At the corner, turn the binding inside out and fold across.*

A  B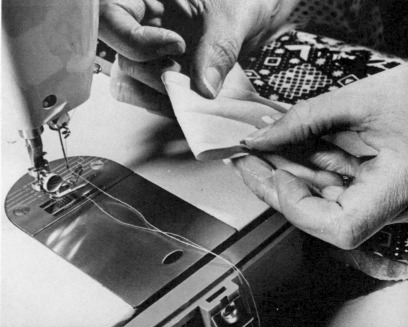

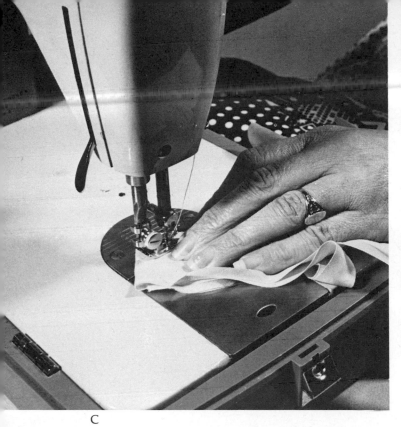

C

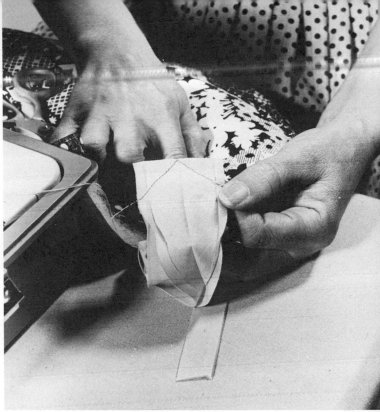

D

C. *Sew an arrow from the centerfold of the binding to its sides.*
D. *How the completed arrow should look.*
E. *Turn it inside-out (right-side out again).*
F. *The completed corner. This is called mitering.*

E

F

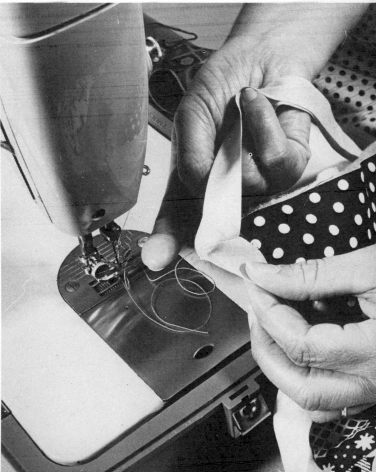

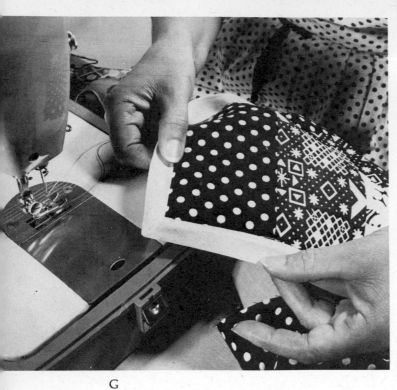

G

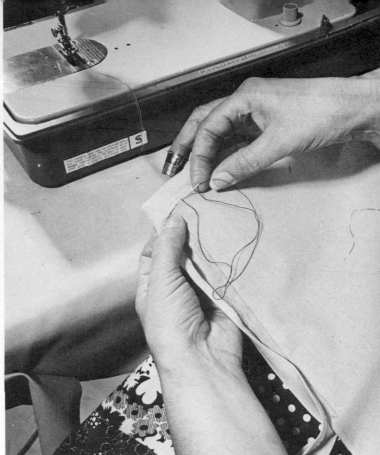

H

G. *Continue sewing to the front of the quilt, mitering each corner, until the entire cover is edged.*

H. *The binding is attached to the rear of the cover by hand-done slip stitches.*

I. *Stitch to the mitered corner.*

J. *Without pausing, continue around the corners, until the binding is completely attached to the cover.*

I

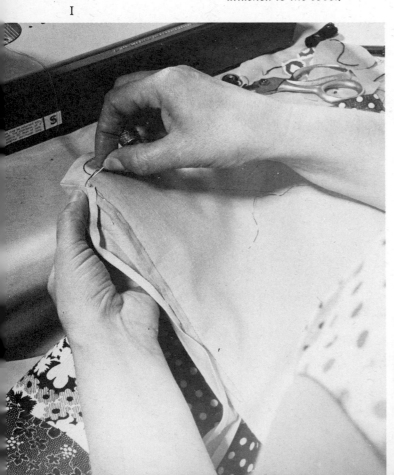

J

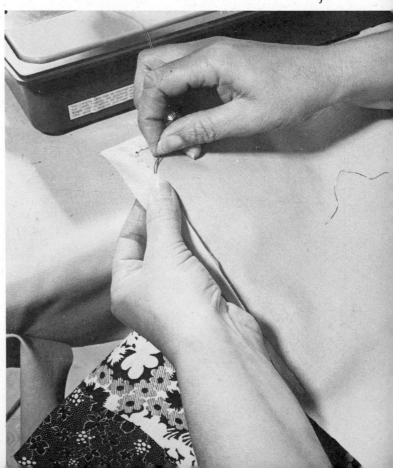

A

B

FIG. 23. *Placing quilt in quilting frame.*

    A. Tacking batting and backing to one side of the quilting frame.
    B. Rolling tacked batting and backing on the side of the frame.
    C. After batting and backing are almost completely rolled, put side back in notch
       and tack the end of the batting and backing to the other side.
    D. Continue rolling the original side until the batting and backing are taut on the
       frame and then slip rolled side back into its notches.

C

D

E. Baste one end of the quilt to the unrolled end of batting and backing.

F. Although it is better to draw the entire quilting pattern beforehand, it is possible to draw it while the quilt is in the frame. For straight lines, always use a ruler. All quilting patterns should be drawn lightly in chalk that will brush off or any similarly erasable substance. Note that pencil will wash out but cannot be removed by dry cleaning.

G. After completing one area of quilting, roll quilt top, batting, and backing on the side of the frame that has not yet been rolled.

H

I

H. *After the completed portion of work is rolled, unfurl enough batting and backing*
from other side to stretch tautly under the new portion of cover to be quilted.
I. *Replace rolled batting and backing in its notch and start quilting again.*

be done while holding the cover in your lap. It is cumbersome, but it does work.

It was a way of life not uncommon in rural America. Unfortunately, it is in many ways inimical to commercialization. Before the marvelous gifts of the women could be organized into something that was income producing, there had to be an understanding of these basic attitudes and traditions. They could not be separated from the craft, for they were responsible for having kept it alive through many generations.

Perhaps, one good reason why Florette Angel and many other early Mountain Artisans organizers were able to perceive local needs and aspirations was that they had been reared in small towns and rural environments. Their points of view had been shaped by a background of town and country rather than large city.

Mountain Artisans came into existence as the result of the confluence of four elements:

1. The existence of real local skills.
2. The need for new channels of employment among low-income people.
3. President Johnson's proclamation of a war on poverty which brought about the Office of Economic Opportunity.
4. A renaissance of interest in American handicrafts.

In the very beginning, Florette Angel provided a major portion of the drive and enthusiasm that brought about this merger. Mrs. Angel was employed in the Arts and Crafts program of the Department of Commerce. The program had produced some very real results. When it was started, in 1963, the reported sales from West Virginia crafts had amounted to $12,000. By 1966, the figure had risen to $250,000. Much of this improvement was due to the annual Mountain State Arts and Crafts Fair, in Ripley, which was jointly sponsored by the Departments of Commerce and Agriculture and the West Virginia Artists and Craftsmen's Guild.

The fair gave many local craftsmen and artists a chance to display and merchandise their wares. It provided them with wholesale contacts that could keep them busy all year. Buyers dealing in handcrafts make the rounds of fairs of this sort in order to find likely products for their customers.

Part of Florette's job was researching local crafts and craftsmen. The purpose of this investigation was to discover which small craft-industries were worthy of (or eligible for) government aid and which independent groups could be organized into cooperatives. A cooperative is a group of craftsmen who share both expenses and earnings. In other words, the workers own the business and derive all of the benefits from their labors. One of the advantages it has over working independently is the ability to market collectively.

One cooperative, sponsored by the Community Action group in its county, had a variety of products for sale but absolutely no idea of how to get them before the public. Responding to a call for help, the Department of Commerce sent Florette Angel. What impressed her most were the remarkable needle skills of the women. Working

A

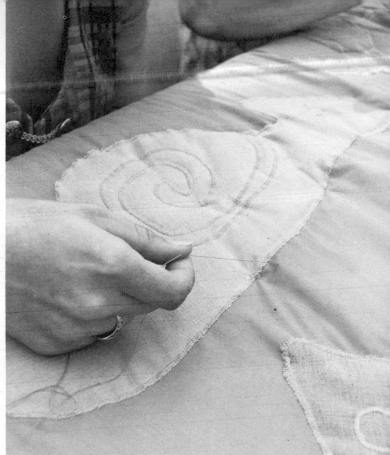

B

Fig. 24. *The quilting stitch.*
   A. *Bring the short quilting needle with knotted sturdy thread up from the bottom of quilt in frame through the backing and batting to the cover surface.*
   B. *Pull it taut.*
   C. *When doing quilting stitches, always keep one hand under the quilt to make certain that the stitches go through all the layers.*
   D. *For quilting, always use a regularly spaced running stitch of as uniform a size as possible.*

C

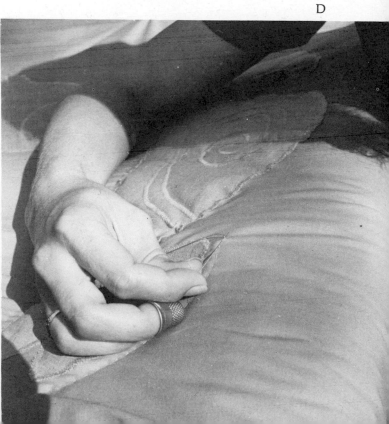

D

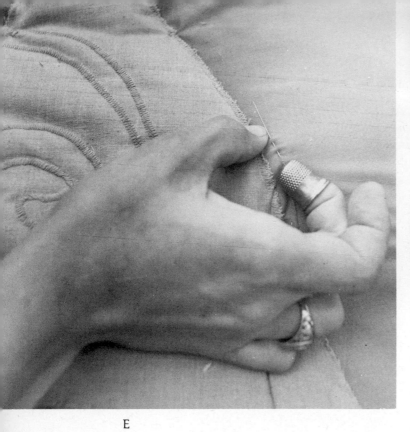

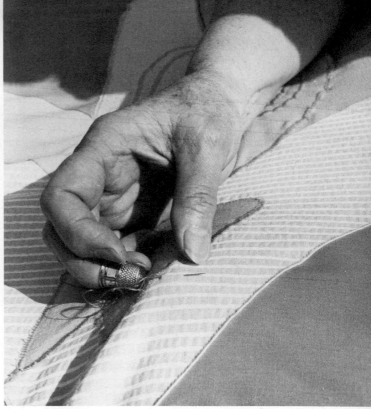

E   F

E. With practice, the proficient quilter can gather three or four stitches at one time.

F. To end a chain of quilting stitches, or to stop to rethread, bring the needle up some small distance away from the quilted line.

G. Snip the thread off as close to the surface as possible. The thread end will disappear without undoing the completed quilting stitches.

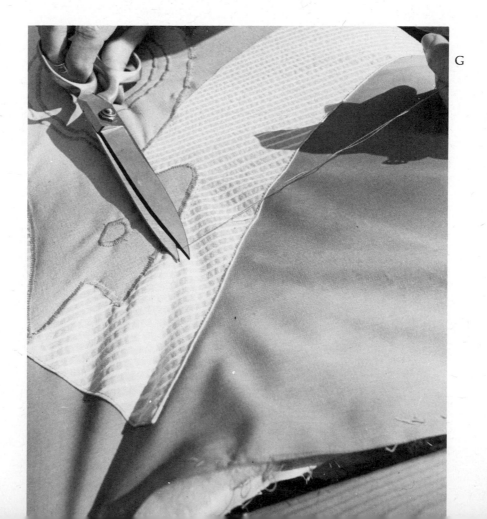

G

50

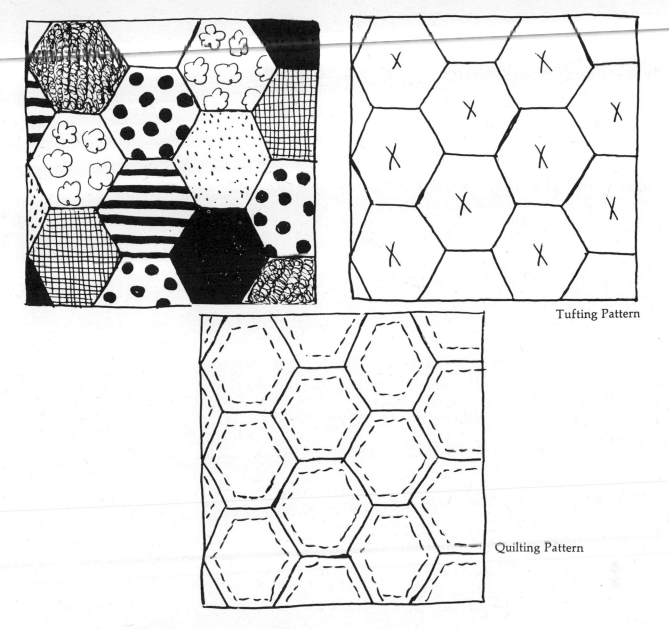

Tufting Pattern

Quilting Pattern

FIG. 25. *Giant Maxigon design, tufting pattern, and quilting pattern.*

in traditional patterns, they often created quilts of great delicacy and surprising sophistication (see Plate III facing page 7).

The problems were many. Obviously, a commercial outlet had to be found. Before that, the group had to obtain the funds to purchase fabric to make enough quilts to interest a potential buyer. There was also the very large question of fair payment for the labor involved. It takes a lot of time to make an intricate quilt. If the quilters were to receive an adequate wage, the price would be too high to compete with machine-made covers and those picked up by itinerant exploiters for a fraction of their worth. The hills abounded with cases of women given the fabrics and a twenty-dollar fee by these unscrupulous types for a quilt that took several weeks of concentrated work to construct.

Florette asked the women if they would be willing to use their skills to make something different. She was very conscious of fashion trends, and what she had in mind was a hostess skirt. Aside from the fact that she judged the time was right for this look in clothes, a skirt would take half the fabric of a cover and could be completed in much less time. It could also be sold for a price that would provide a fair return on the labor involved.

When the women of the cooperative agreed, Florette contacted a Charleston merchant and asked if he would be willing to buy the skirts. He agreed to order six on a trial basis.

With no designer to help, no concept of sizing, no pattern, and no precedent for construction, Florette returned to the group with great enthusiasm. It was so easy, she assured them. Why, all they had to do was figure out what to do. After much trial and error, they finally came up with three skirts. Florette said, "It was like the blind leading the blind. Why, I didn't even know how to use a sewing machine."

The skirts sold, a fact that still amazes Mary Lee Bond, one of the original Mountain Artisans board members: "With what they knew about sizing, the ladies who bought them must have had mighty peculiar figures."

It was only later that the cooperative was able to come up with styles as sophisticated as the Sun Up skirt. (See fig. 26 page 53.) But it was these initial experiments that proved there was a market for such items and made all that followed possible.

Basically, the Sun Up skirt is nothing more complicated than an experiment in piecing. Once that basic has been mastered, the rest is easy.

From the time that the Mountain Artisans introduced their first pieced skirts, these skirts have been a part of the fashion lexicon

FIG. 26. *The Sun Up skirt*.

that never seems to date. Women who own the original designs are still wearing them years later. Sun Up is a particularly pretty and timeless example of the genre. It's also delightfully easy to make. If there's any hesitation about just plunging in and doing it from scratch, simply buy any commercial pattern for a long gathered skirt and use it as a guide. But it really is simple to make by following the Mountain Artisans' instructions.

Four contrasting colored or patterned fabrics are necessary. Purchase two yards of fabric #1 (the light polka dot in fig. 26), two yards of fabric #2 (the solid stripe, fig. 26), three-quarters of a yard of fabric #3 (the solid triangle, fig. 26), and two yards of fabric #4 (the dark tiny dot, fig. 26). Also purchase four yards of ribbon and thirteen yards of ½" rickrack. If a lining is desired, buy 6 yds. of a fabric that is harmonious with the other four fabrics (it might even be one of them) and cut a rectangle measuring 44" by 72".

It is possible to make an endless number of skirts, all different, by changing the colors and designs of the fabric, ribbon, and rickrack.

From fabric #1, cut *four* 2¾" by 72" strips and *two* 8¾" by 72" strips. Reserve the rest.

From fabric #2, cut *two* 4¾" by 72" strips. (It's possible to buy less than a full yard of this fabric, but then there will be piecing seams in order to make the 72" strip.) Now follow the instructions given in figure 27 pages 55–57.

It was about this time that Sharon Percy Rockefeller became interested in the group. As both the daughter and the wife of men who were devoting their energies to public service, she was naturally interested in community action programs, especially from the point of view of providing employment for limited-income rural women.

Sharon had been teaching kindergarten in a poor community and had already discovered that the West Virginians were a proud and admirable people. In many ways, they seemed to be living in another era, one in which it was still possible to adhere to original American standards and values. Although many did not have much education, what they had in terms of intrinsic principles she often found more praiseworthy than the facts her more sophisticated contemporaries had learned from books.

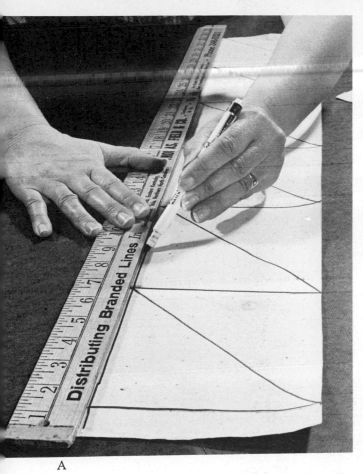

A

B

FIG. 27. Construction of the Sun Up skirt.
  A. Draw a series of triangles on a long strip of paper. In order to do this, you will
     need a pattern for a right-angle triangle with each of the short sides measuring
     4" (⅜" must be added on all sides for a seam allowance).*
  B. Pin the paper pattern to the fabrics to be cut into triangles.
  C. First, cut along the parallel lines.
  D. Then, cut along the diagonals.

  *To make any triangles with a ⅜" seam allowance, draw and cut squares 1⅛"
  larger on all sides than the desired triangle. Cut them in half diagonally. This will
  give triangles with ⅜" seam allowances. For the 4" triangle, the square is 5⅛".
  For a 2" triangle, the square would be 3⅛", etc.

C

D

E

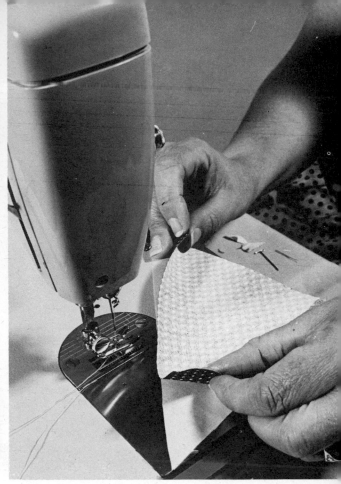

F

E. Continue the cutting until there are 54 triangles of each fabric. Cut triangles and pattern.

F. Using the ⅜" seam allowance along the diagonal, sew a square of one triangle of each fabric.

G. Using the ⅜" seam allowance along the sides, sew the squares together so that the fabrics alternate. Continue doing this until there are three rows of a total of 36 triangles each.

H. Rule and cut seven 2¾" by 72" strips from fabric #1; from fabric #2, rule off and cut two 4¾" by 72" strips and one 2¾" by 72" strip; from fabric #4, rule and cut one 6¾" by 72" strip.

G

H

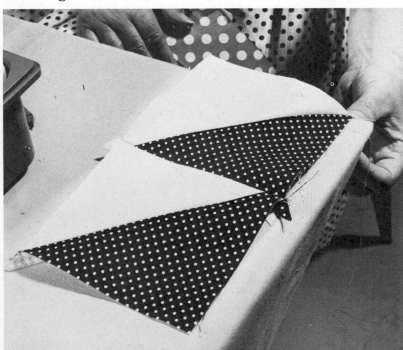

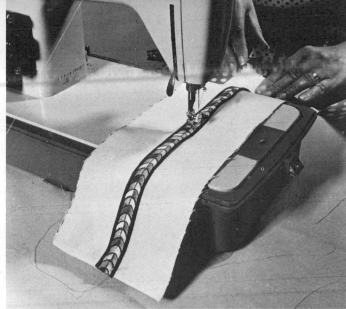

I

J

I. Cut the ribbon in half. Cut six 72" strips of rickrack (reserve the rest for the waistband). The rickrack is used along the center of all the strips of Fabric #1, except the very top one, and the ribbon along the center of the two wider strips of Fabric #2.

J. Start sewing the ribbon and rickrack in place.

K. Start assembling the skirt, using the rows of triangles and those of fabric.

L. The pieces of Sun Up skirt begin to take shape.

Starting from the bottom and using figure 28 as a guide, sew the strip of fabric #4 to a strip of fabric #1 to a row of triangles, to a strip of fabric #1 to a strip of fabric #2, and so on, ending with the narrow strip of fabric #2 (that has no ribbon on it) and the remaining strip of fabric #1 (without rickrack). The completed rectangle should measure 72" by 42¾". Iron it to flatten all the seams.

Close the rectangle with a back seam and insert a zipper in the top. If a lining is desired, make it of a light fabric of a complementary color. Make a waistband from some of the remaining fabric #1 and gather the skirt and lining into it. Complete by covering the seam connecting waistband and skirt with the reserved rickrack and hemming.

K

L

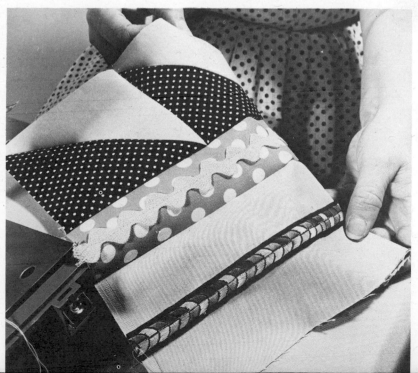

Sharon wanted to help and put Florette in touch with the business manager of Parish-Hadley, a firm she knew had been experimenting with quilted fabric in home decoration.

The business manager described a small-scale fabric utilizing shades like hot pink, poison green, and orange. He concluded, "If you understand the shades I mean, you're twelve steps ahead of anybody else making quilted fabrics."

One of the problems his firm was encountering was that every time they ordered an item from quilting groups, the colors they wanted were so alien to the tradition that they had to go down to supervise the construction. This added considerably to the price.

Florette convinced him to let them try. He reluctantly agreed to order three yards to be used for covering writing portfolios. For the original materials, from which this high-style fabric would be fashioned, the women went to a local cut-rate store, the K-Mart, and bought forty-five different patterns in ¼ yards lengths.

At the time, they had no designer but, although nobody is quite sure how they managed to do it, they came up with a quilted design that was so successful that Parish-Hadley subsequently ordered an additional 30 yards which they used to upholster a variety of things, including some wonderful Chippendale chairs.

When an order came in for six more skirts, Florette Angel, who is by nature given to leaping fifteen or twenty steps ahead of any practical considerations, had visions of a statewide industry. It was obvious only to her that they were on the threshold of revolutionizing the world of fashion and home furnishings.

In the spring of 1968, however, it did not even seem likely that the small order for skirts could be filled. The cooperative did not have the money to buy the necessary materials, and the Department of Commerce flatly refused to advance it. They had no money in the Arts and Crafts budget except for staff and travel.

As far as the government was concerned, the group was a bad risk. They did not have any managerial setup nor did they have the means of reaching a large market. To tell the truth, the women were not interested in those things. They only wanted to earn some extra money by using their skills in a constructive way.

Florette would not be put down. By the autumn of that year, she had gathered a group of community-minded people including Governor Hulett Smith's wife, Sharon Rockefeller, an attorney named Page Henley, Jr., Brent Galyean, Mary Lee Bond, Clark Tierney, and Nancy Knapp. They met in the governor's mansion, where Florette presented her plans for the formation of a statewide cooperative corporation. The group decided to go along with her. They proposed to form a nonprofit, nonshareholding organization, because these were the conditions by which they could obtain a state charter enabling them to solicit funds that would be tax-deductible to the contributors. A prospectus for the charter would have to be submitted to the state government, and for that, a name for the cooperative would have to be found. Many names were submitted and rejected. The search for the proper designation was so irritating that suggestions began to be put forward that could not be printed in a newspaper let alone set forth on a legal document. Finally, they hit upon Mountain Artisans. None of the original group is quite sure how it came about but, once the two words were spoken, they knew it had the right ring. It was neither too folksy nor too sophisticated. Mountain Artisans sounded true and sincere. It was what it was all about.

While the Mountain Artisans group was being formed, possible designers were being canvassed. There were two qualifications necessary for the person who would eventually create the original Mountain Artisans "look." He or she must be able to turn out a line reflecting the special quality that had provided the original artistic inspiration for the organization. This led directly to the second qualification: the designer must have a natural sympathy for the people, the area, the cause.

The search began and ended with a group of local artists who agreed to donate their time and talents to the effort. Among them, there was a young woman named Dorothy Weatherford.

Mrs. Weatherford was born in Tennessee. Her mother's family had come from the Appalachian region of Kentucky where for generations the women had been making quilts.

Before the Mountain Artisans more or less took over her artistic life, she had experimented in using patchwork as part of a series of paintings. She had often exhibited, had won awards, and was generally considered a promising young painter, but the quilting tradition was very much a part of her background and heritage.

Because of her natural sympathy for the project and her feelings for the medium, Dorothy Weatherford soon emerged as the chief designer for the group and was almost completely responsible for the distinctive look that was originated by the Mountain Artisans. More than any other designer in the world, she has made the patch a status symbol in high fashion and home furnishings.

In addition to her highly original work, she has often worked within old patterns using new fabrics and arrangements of them to create new looks. Slashed Diagonal is one of this group (see fig. 28 page 60). The square blocks are composed of two triangles pieced together. This is the basis of many traditional patterns. In essence, the previously mentioned Old Maid's Puzzle (see fig. 16 page 19) is only an amplification of this.

The first step in Slashed Diagonal is to draw a right-angle triangle with the short sides measuring 6″ each. Then add ⅜″ seam allowance to all three sides and cut.

Eight different fabrics give an effective color and design range for your quilt.

Determine the number of blocks needed to make the quilt. This is done by dividing the length by six, the width by six, multiplying these two numbers, then doubling the answer. If the measurements of your quilt aren't evenly divisible by six, you must round them off. For example, a twin bed coverlet measuring 67″ by 110″ should be rounded off to 66″ by 108″. To determine the number of triangles

FIG. 28. *Slashed Diagonal*.

One
Block

Six Inches
Square

A

FIG. 29. *Cutting out triangles for the Slashed Diagonal quilt.*
   A. *Place the triangle pattern in a corner of the fabric and outline it.*
   B. *Flip the pattern over on the diagonal.*

B

C

C. With the same diagonal line as the first triangle, outline the other two sides to complete a square.

D. Cut out the square and cut it in half along the diagonal line. If care is used, this entire process can be done with several layers of fabric.

D

PLATE IX. *Quilt illustrating use of subtle tones and juxtaposition of textured materials.*

PLATE X. *The Rockefeller quilt.*

PLATE XI. *Spinning Wheel*
quilt.

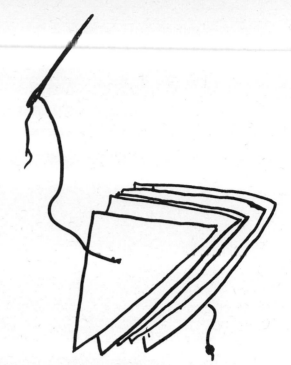

FIG. 30. *Stringing fabric pieces.*

needed, divide 66 by 6, which equals 11, and 108 by 6, which equals 18. Multiply 11 times 18 times 2, which equals 396 triangles. Using eight fabrics, you need approximately 50 triangles in each color. Cut the triangles (see fig. 29 pages 61–62).

After cutting, string each set of fabrics on a thread (see fig. 30 page 63). This will keep them separated and from going astray.

The next step is to start piecing along the diagonal to form 6 ¾″ squares of two triangles. For Slashed Diagonal, there are only two things to keep in mind. All of the diagonal lines in the blocks go in the same direction, from upper left to lower right. No two fabrics of the same pattern should ever touch each other.

For quilting, assemble the batting and backing with the top. One can tuft, as seen in the pattern in figure 32 on page 65, or one can quilt by putting the pieces in the quilting frame and stitching (see fig. 33 page 65), following the quilting pattern of running along the perimeter of each block.

There are all sorts of variations possible on the basic Slashed Diagonal. In one (see fig. 34 page 65), the block is increased to four small blocks pieced into the larger one. This means all eight fabrics are used in each unit. The diagonals are placed so that they meet in points at both sides and top and bottom, forming a diamond. In piecing the large blocks, the only thing to watch is that at no point should the same fabrics touch.

Tufting is used to quilt with the tufts placed exactly as they are in Slashed Diagonal, at the corner of each small block within the larger blocks.

FIG. 31. *Variations on the Slashed Diagonal. In the smaller piece, many fabrics are used with the diagonals all going in one direction. In the larger piece, only four fabrics are used, and an abstract geometric pattern emerges by altering direction and placement in both the blocks and lines of blocks.*

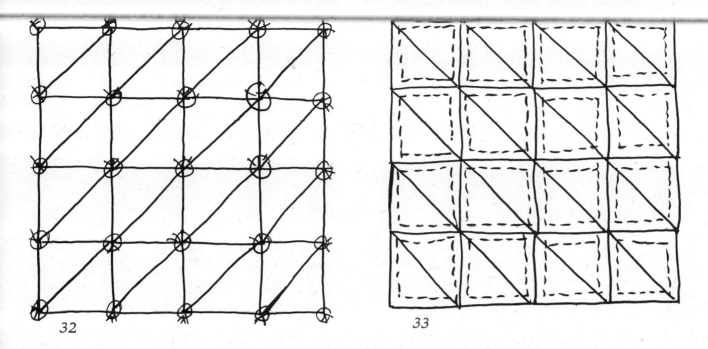

FIG. 32. *Tufting pattern for Slashed Diagonal. Combine quilt top with batting and and backing, place in hoop, and tuft.*

FIG. 33. *Quilting pattern for Slashed Diagonal. If preferred, the cover can be placed in a frame and quilted. Bind with desired width and color of seam binding.*

FIG. 34. *Slashed Diagonal variation.*

FIG. 35. *Giant Tripping Triangles (variation of Slashed Diagonal).*

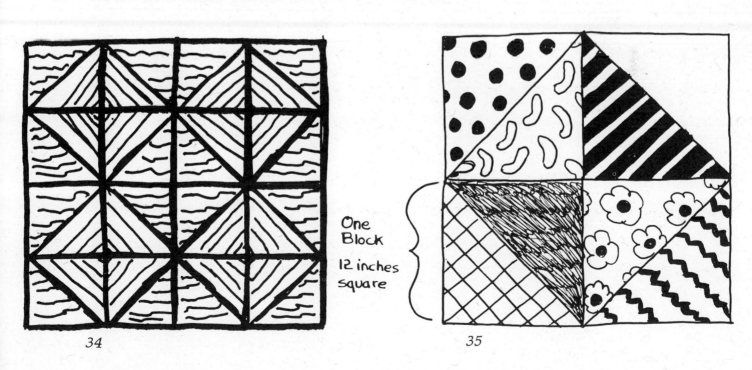

One
Block

12 inches
square

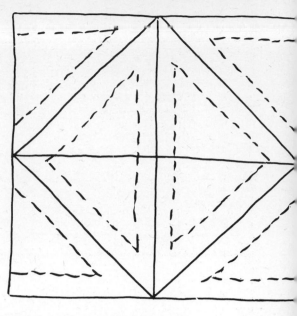

FIG. 36. *Quilting pattern for Giant Tripping Triangles.*

For Giant Tripping Triangles, another variation, see figure 35 page 65. The size of the triangle is increased to 12″ (with a ⅜″ seam allowance). To make a pattern, draw a right-angle triangle with both short sides measuring 12″. Then add ⅜″ seam allowance to all three sides. Again, eight fabrics are used to make the giant block of four smaller blocks, and the diagonals meet in points. In this case, however, the placement of triangles is rigidly controlled, so that the same fabric falls in exactly the same position in each block.

See figure 36 on page 66 for the quilting pattern for Giant Tripping Triangles, which is stitched in a quilting frame.

By November 1968, the Mountain Artisans had their charter, their purpose, and their designer. They wanted not only to preserve the mountain crafts, but also to modernize and reshape them to suit contemporary living patterns. Most of all, they wanted to provide a marketing outlet for the quilters in their cooperative. It was this last ambition that set them apart from other groups seeking to benefit native craftsmen—groups which simply wanted to get them working, without much thought given to how to keep them working by creating a steady demand for their products.

For all the dedication with which they worked at the project, that first winter season of their existence was one of great discontent. It very often looked as if it would also be their last season. There was no money in the till. They applied to every foundation they could think of without any success. Sharon even applied to one of the Rockefeller family's foundations, where one would have thought that her name might carry some weight. For all the good it did, she might as well have been called Mrs. Smith.

Somehow, mostly through contributions from board members, they managed to amass enough money to make a very limited collection of sample models, all designed by Dorothy Weatherford, for showing in the spring of 1969.

The fabrics were all purchased in the remnants shop in Charleston. The women who made the items worked more on faith than wages. As a matter of fact, everybody was working on faith. There was not a single paid member on the staff.

Because there was no money for rent, the mailing address was Phil Angel's office, the designing was done by Dorothy at home and the organizational work at the Angel home, which they called the Tree House. As the group so often found themselves up one, it was a very apt name for their headquarters.

In March 1969, a group of Artisans decided to go to New York with what they euphemistically called their spring line. There was no money for transportation, so Dorothy's parents financed her trip, Nancy Knapp financed herself, and the Department of Commerce was conned into financing Florette.

That first collection consisted of six skirts, one quilt, a couple of pillows, and some fabric. With that scant inventory, the intrepid pioneers reversed history and went East determined to carve a new territory for themselves.

In Plate V, facing page 22, Sharon Rockefeller is seen wearing one of those first pieced skirts. The classic combination of four fabrics very simply pieced in stripes and triangles makes it as fashionable today as it was when it was first made. Although they did not know it at the time, this timelessness was to become the Mountain Artisans' secret weapon with consumers. It was comforting to know that an expensive, handmade garment could justify its price by its longevity.

CHAPTER FOUR

"Pretty as a picture, this quilt is. I only use it for special occasions."
—LINCOLN COUNTY QUILTER

THE Mountain Artisans' first descent upon New York was during those hectic weeks when important buyers from all over the country visit the big city to view the summer collections of all the designers and manufacturers. They took the least expensive room at the Gotham Hotel, because they had been told that it was one of the centers for the out-of-towners.

When they started to unpack, Nancy Knapp asked, "Where's the closet?"

Florette looked around the very tiny room and replied dryly, "I think we must be standing in it."

Well, they were at the hub of things, the place where all the action was—and it was terribly exciting—but they had not the faintest idea of what to do next. Did they simply sit around and wait for buyers to drop in? Did they call people? If so, which people?

Heaven must really protect the innocents of this world, Heaven and Diana Vreeland.

Mrs. Vreeland was the estimable editor of *Vogue* magazine, and the wheel of wheels in the fashion world. When she decreed to her hapless readers that something was "in," it was *in*, or they were *out*.

The people at Parish-Hadley had set up an appointment for the women to see Mrs. Vreeland. Clutching two of the new skirts, Florette, Dorothy, and Nancy were conducted through a labyrinth of offices, cluttered with women of unbelievable chic, until they found themselves before the door to the inner sanctum. As they started forward, a secretary held up her hand like a policeman at a traffic intersection.

"No! Mrs. Vreeland sees no more than two people at a time." She pointed to Dorothy and Florette. "You."

Nancy shrugged and handed over the skirt that she was carrying. "Don't forget," she whispered. "Tell her about the women—and what it means to them."

As Florette nodded, the secretary said crisply, "Don't say a word until you're spoken to. She doesn't like chatterboxes."

When the woman said "she," there were italics in her voice. Florette and Dorothy timidly entered the office. A jointed bough of a woman rested an elbow on her desk, supporting her chin on a bejeweled fist, and peered at them. They smiled nervously and, not knowing what else to do, thrust the skirts toward the formidable creature.

There were five minutes of silence that seemed like an eternity. While Mrs. Vreeland studied the garments, Dorothy cast furtive glances around the room. It was red, very red—everything was red except the column of black crepe hunched over the desk.

It was like having an audience with the Dalai Lama. In the gloom, Florette was even certain that she could detect the odor of incense. Finally, the seeress spoke. "Girls, you've got something that could be great. It's going to be rough. You're going to have lots of hard times ahead. But if you hang in, you can make it."

Florette and Dorothy exchanged incredulous glances and felt twelve-feet tall. The room wasn't red and gloomy. It was glowing with brilliant shafts of sunshine. Diana Vreeland had approved and, with the sure touch of Ali Baba, she opened doors for the Artisans. Her staff provided important names. They made calls setting up appointments. Her italicized secretary said, "We're arranging for you to see *the* people, the *important* people."

If there were any other people of consequence, her tone instantly dismissed them. And, from the point of view of high fashion, she was right. Skirts not unlike the Jungle Bouquet (see fig. 37 page 70) had passed inspection by the douane of couture. As with all lasting designs, the secret was in its simplicity.

To duplicate it, purchase a commercial pattern for an A-line skirt with no front center seam and enough solid fabric to construct it (an ivory corduroy is very smart). Cut it and lay it out and follow the instruction in figure 38 on pages 71–73.

A pattern for a little bolero jacket can be purchased and con-

FIG. 37. *The Jungle Bouquet skirt*.

70

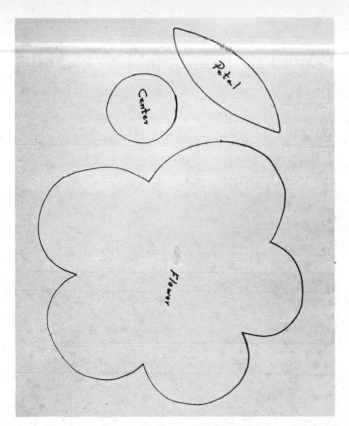

A

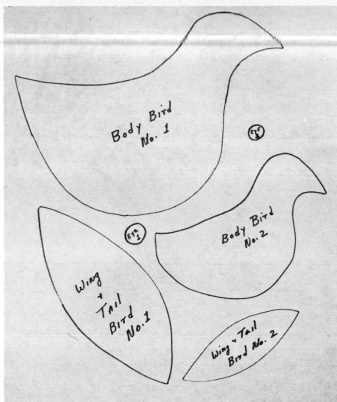

B

Fig. 38. *Construction of the Jungle Bouquet skirt.*

A. *After purchasing and cutting your A-line skirt pattern, on cardboard, draw the patterns for flowers, centers, and leaves for 10" and 8" flowers. If uncertain about measurements, draw a circle of that diameter and sketch the flower within it. Pictured here, a drawing for pattern of a large flower, petal, and center.*

B. *Draw the patterns for two birds, their wings, and their eyes. The larger bird should be about 10" long and the smaller about 8" long.*

C. *Cutting out the bird patterns.*

D. *The completely cut patterns.*

C

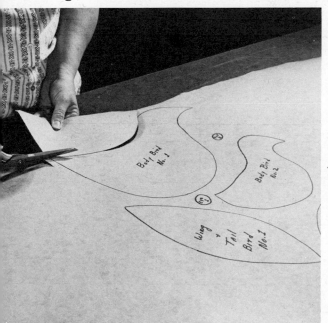

D

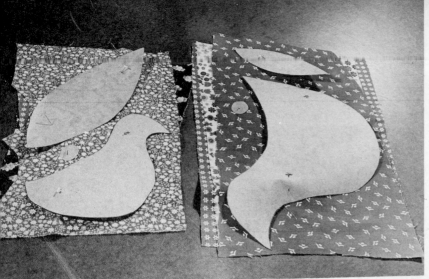

E

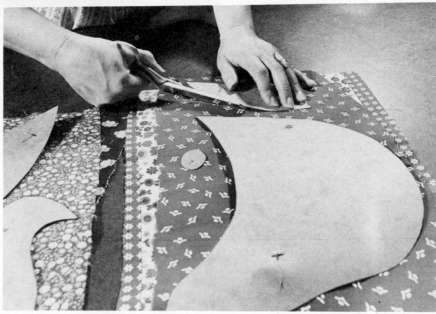

F

E. Pin the patterns to as many fabrics as pieces desired for the appliqué. For a
   richly appliquéd skirt, cut a great many. For an understated garment, use fewer.
F. Cut around the patterns through the layers of fabric.
G. The cardboard pattern pieces with fabrics ready to be appliquéd.
   Repeat with the flower patterns and make the floral appliqués.

G

H. Lay out the skirt body, move the appliqués around until the positioning is pleasing, and then pin them in place.

I. Zigzag stitch the appliqués in place on the skirt.

J. Zigzagging can also be done by hand. After all the pieces are zigzag appliquéd to the skirt body, complete the skirt according to the pattern instructions. Sew the appliqués that overlap the seam right into the seam and snip off excess bits.

   Final Note: Don't worry about overlapping appliqués. Zigzag one over the other in the position that is most pleasing.

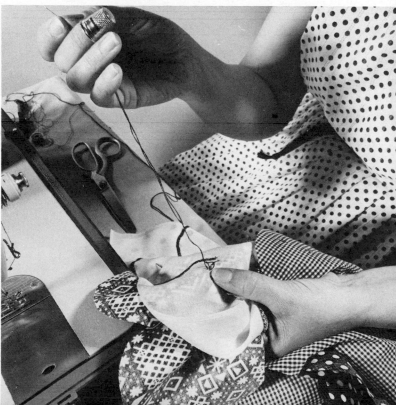

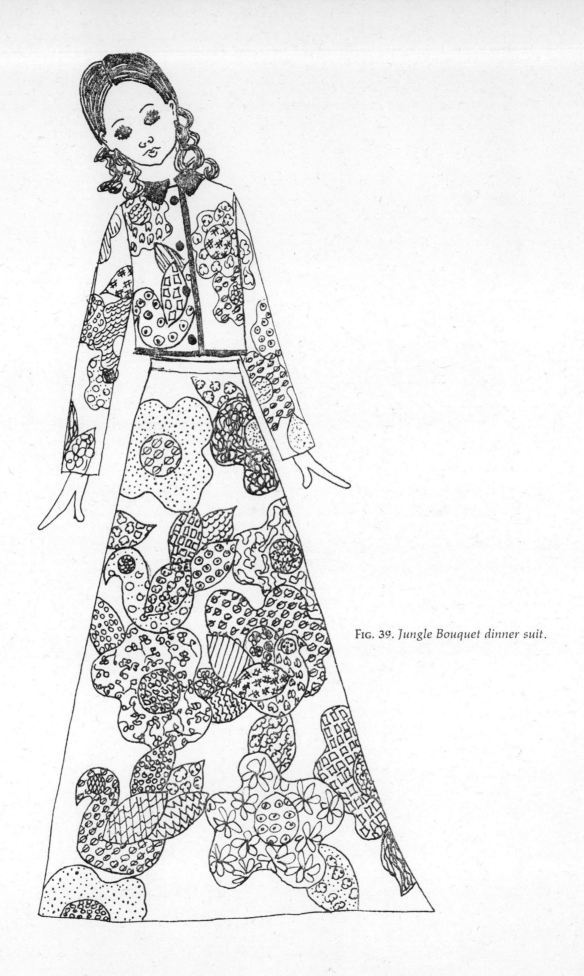

FIG. 39. *Jungle Bouquet dinner suit.*

74

structed in exactly the same way to make a smashing dinner suit as seen in figure 39.

New York was wonderful to the Mountain Artisans. The fashion magazines started photographing the clothes, and those devoted to home furnishings did the quilts and pillows. They got in to see all of the important designers with the greatest of ease. It was true that they were being seen as a favor to Diana Vreeland, but these great names were unfailingly courteous and helpful. Two were more than that. Donald Brooks ordered some of the fabric, and Oscar de La Renta became so excited by the possibilities that he began to cut out pieces of material and pin them together, designing two pieced fabrics before their eyes. He worked so swiftly that Florette and Nancy were worried that he might swallow the pins. When he ordered both designs, the women were still more worried about the pins: If they fell out in transit, no one at the cooperative would ever be able to reassemble de La Renta's designs.

For his next collection, de La Renta did two magnificent gowns made out of the Mountain Artisans fabric. The gowns got standing ovations at his press showing, and he generously gave full credit to the Artisans. The dresses were far too expensive to sell, but they more than compensated for their cost in the amount of publicity they garnered. They were photographed and reproduced everywhere.

The story has an ironic conclusion. After touring the country, the sample gowns ended up in a store in California, where they were seen by a woman from Charleston who adored them, not knowing where the fabric was made. Even at the discounted prices for sample models, they were still too expensive, and she regretfully left for home without buying them.

Later, when the dresses went on sale, and the store notified the woman, she ordered one and, after being widely photographed in her fantastic de La Renta, was told that the luxuriant material had been made in the hills of her home state.

Despite the excitement and publicity, there was a strange lack of interest among the buyers in the big stores. The women consoled themselves with the knowledge that they were becoming famous in the small town of New York pacesetters. This rather select group had taken the Mountain Artisans as one of their own. Florette was certain that, before long, the rest of the country would follow. After all, these terribly smart women did set the standards for style.

In the meantime, it seemed a wise idea to limit the publicity. They did not want to exhaust the outlets for mass communication before they had found their market. When Judy Klemesrud of the *New York Times* called and asked to do a story, they hesitated. Miss Klemesrud was astonished. Nobody had ever hesitated before about a *Times* story. As a matter of fact, everybody in the fashion and home furnishings business begged for them. She finally asked, "You have heard of the *New York Times*, haven't you?"

Only one big store, Neiman Marcus, came through with an order. What about the others? With all the talk about the Artisans, why weren't they breaking down the doors? Why weren't they even knocking at the doors?

They made the rounds of all of the New York stores to no avail. Toward the end of their stay, they discovered why they were meeting with so much sales resistance. One of the buyers looked at their samples. They could see that he was genuinely excited by them and began to feel hopeful. Inexplicably, he turned them down. Nancy asked, "Would you mind telling us why you're not ordering? You obviously like what you've seen."

"The stuff's great. Just terrific. But I wouldn't touch it."

"Why? Tell us—why."

"You're from West Virginia."

The women were flabbergasted. They looked at him as if he were mad. What did he have against West Virginia? Why, it had even been on the Yankee side during the Civil War.

He continued, "I'll tell you. Another woman from your state was up to see me with quilted things. Not as good looking as yours. But darn nice. I knew I could sell them. She was nice, too. I gave her a lovely order. That was over a year ago. I'm still waiting for delivery."

That explained it. The Mountain Artisans was not the only West Virginia group trying to help women of limited incomes by building up sewing cooperatives. Although it was an expensive lesson, they decided then and there that, when they made their breakthrough, they would guarantee delivery and quality control. Because of this, they were the group with the best organization almost from their inception.

The setback did not lessen their enthusiasm. When they returned to Charleston, they were elated. They excitedly reported to the board about the great interest everybody had demonstrated.

Vogue was falling all over itself trying to be helpful. *Mademoiselle*, too. They really were on their way. The Artisans was a bandwagon with the whole fashion world hopping on. Then one of the board members, Mary Lee Bond, asked, "That's all very well, but, in dollars and cents, how many orders did you get?"

Florette beamed. "$7,000."

Several members exchanged glances and then turned their eyes upward toward the good Lord. One observed, "We've got four sewing groups waiting to go to work. Now, how are you going to keep them all busy with $7,000 worth of orders? They can finish that in a couple of weeks."

The group's attorney, Page Henley, asked, "Where are you going to get the money to buy the materials necessary to make even that much?"

Florette answered brightly, "We'll get a loan."

"From whom?"

"Any of the banks will be happy to give it to us. After all, we're on our way."

There was a collective sigh, and the unasked question— "Where?"—was almost audible in the room.

It was during this period that many of the original boosters and members of the Mountain Artisans began to drop by the wayside. They dismissed the whole project as an Angelic dream, for it was only Florette and Phil Angel who really kept the faith and, through their courage and zeal, managed to hold together what remained of the organization.

The immediate need was $5,000 to enable the group to complete the orders. After being rejected by every other loan company and bank in the region, Florette finally called William Shearer, of the Kanawha Banking and Trust Company. Their motto was "Person-to-Person Banking." Shearer had been among those who originally had met at the Governor's mansion and, person to person, Florette told him that he would have to come up with the loan, or the Mountain Artisans would have to fold its quilts and steal silently into the West Virginia night.

The banker was sympathetic, and he had always believed that businessmen were looking for ways to demonstrate their social responsibility. Well, he thought, if there was ever a chance for him to stand up and be counted for his belief, this was it. He decided to go forward with the loan, regarding it as a charitable contribution and never thinking that he would ever be repaid.

The sewing groups set to work at filling the initial orders. The Artisans even found an official headquarters. Jay Rockefeller had leased a building when running for Secretary of State of West Virginia, and at the request of his wife, Sharon, he turned over the attic to the Artisans.

Dorothy optimistically set to work on another line. Charming works like the Butterfly quilt (see fig. 40 page 79) seemed to pour effortlessly from her creative storehouse.

Eight or nine cottons in shades of pink and lavender are cut to make the butterflies in this quilt. After moving them around on the background and finding a pleasing position, the quilters pin or baste them in long stitches.

The butterflies and parts are hand- or machine-appliquéd. Cover, batting, and backing (for this, a pink cotton chintz would be pretty) are assembled, put in the quilting frame, and hand quilted in stitches outlining the appliqués.

The quilt is finished off with pink binding.

Hope for the future was the keynote at the Artisans. When Florette had to make a choice between her job with the Department of Commerce and her work with the Mountain Artisans, she opted for the Artisans. She was not alone in her dedication. Dorothy and Brent were with her, devoting as much of their time and effort as possible.

Volunteers started to appear on the scene to help. Perhaps the most valuable was a former Vista worker named Claudia Schecter.

Fig. 40. *Butterfly quilt. This coverlet, perfect for a twin-sized bed in a girl's room, is an example of simplicity merged with a sense of whimsy. The background is solid white cotton chintz. The patterns for the bold, easily drawn butterflies of various sizes and shapes, along with the details for their wings, are sketched and cut from cardboard or heavy paper.*

Claudia had enormous experience in field work and group organization. She was to prove invaluable in keeping contact with the widespread sewing groups. It was a job that often entailed driving six or seven hours a day.

Although all of the groups were composed of excellent needlewomen, who had been working together as units before they joined the Mountain Artisans, they had to be trained in the Artisans' system of quality control, shown the new patterns and, most of all, impressed with the necessity of meeting production deadlines.

In those early days, when work was far from plentiful, Claudia also did a great deal of just visiting, of hand-holding, of listening to problems, of making certain that the women kept the faith in that dark period when faith seemed to be all they had to keep.

For all of the problems, optimism remained high. A funding proposal outlining their aims and needs was drafted. The staff felt certain that, once those with the power to help saw what their intentions were, help would be forthcoming.

Although nobody was being paid, an organization was taking shape. They had a great group of women in Charleston and wonderful sewing groups in the hills. They had a dedicated Board of Directors. They had a home. They were in the news. They had orders to fill.

The drowsy, moist heat of the warm months settled in the Kanawha Valley. The attic was often stifling. But nobody seemed to mind. The heat of their fervor was fiercer. They felt that they were on their way.

Actually, it was the beginning of a summer of a discontent as disheartening as they had experienced in the winter.

CHAPTER FIVE

"There are times a quilt's a way of sayin' 'welcome'—a quilt for a new neighbor, or a new bride, or a new baby. We been doin' that sort of thing all our lives."

—Lincoln County quilter

During that summer of 1969, the Mountain Artisans produced two things in great quantity: dedication and hard work. Dorothy continued to turn out marvelous designs that more than fulfilled the promise of her first scant collection. Florette was omnipresent, lifting everybody's spirits with her contagious faith in the future. With the help of three volunteers, Claudia was doing secretarial work, drafting patterns, and fund raising.

The letters continued to go out to foundations, and the rejections again came back from them. The only hope of raising money was by getting a grant from the Office of Economic Opportunity. Claudia played a key role, staying after hours to make phone calls, following up every lead they got, assuring everybody that, if they got the funding, they would follow the OEO rules.

By June, there was some inkling that the OEO might be receptive, but it still seemed to many members of the Board as if they had reached the end of the road. There was barely enough money to complete the orders on hand and neither new money nor new orders in sight.

Page Henley, Mary Lee Bond, and Sharon Rockefeller met privately to discuss the situation. Although their common sense told them that the project was doomed, their admiration for the purpose of the group and for the spirit of the women was an uncommon phenomenon. They could not bring themselves to desert and entered into a solemn pact to stay with it until January 1970.

Mary Lee took over as president, despite the fact that her husband, who was a clever businessman, read the reports and declared that it was impossible to turn the organization into a going concern. He was not alone in this opinion. Everybody with any business experience said that it was impossible.

But the people most deeply involved determined to keep at it. It was not a question of stubbornness, of proving the others were wrong. That did not enter into it. It was a question of faith. And faith could move mountains—even those stone-hearted mountains of West Virginia.

Co-existent with the troubles, there was pleasure in the creative nature of the project. There was no doubt that the very special Mountain Artisans look was coming into existence. It would often be copied by other groups but never quite duplicated, for nobody else had the very special approach and talents of their designer. As soon as one group of patterns was copied, another was born, and all within the framework of a fresh examination of the ancient craft of quilting.

Dorothy often took old and traditional patterns and revitalized them through an unorthodox use of color and the juxtaposition of fabrics. One of the most beautiful of the old patterns, on which she worked variations, is the Fence Rail (see Plate VI facing page 22).

Quilters enjoy working on the Fence Rail; it goes quickly and is very easy to make. Because it takes only one small pattern piece, it is one of those quilts where the cutting can be done anywhere, even on a train or bus. That also goes for some of the stitching, which if the quilter chooses, can be done by hand.

On cardboard, draw and cut a rectangular pattern measuring 6¾" by 3¼". This will give a 6" by 2½" piece with ⅜" seam allowance all around.

Use a minimum of eight different fabrics. It takes 50 blocks to make a square yard of Fence Rail quilt. One can also cut about 50 blocks from a square yard of fabric. Divide the number of fabrics to be used into the total square yardage of the quilt to be made to find the number of yards of each fabric that will be necessary. Now follow the directions given in figure 41 on pages 83–84.

A

B

FIG. 41. Instructions for making the Fence Rail quilt.
    A. Comparing fabrics to be used to see how they complement each other.
    B. Layer the fabrics so that the straight grains all go in the same direction. Place
        the pattern piece on top, so that the long side is on the straight grain. Outline
        it on the top fabric.
    C. Continue outlining, laying pattern side on side, and cut.
    D. Start piecing in a zigzag fashion. One can either piece an entire row, using the
        ⅜" seam allowance to join the pieces, or one can make blocks which are later
        sewn together to make the quilt.

C

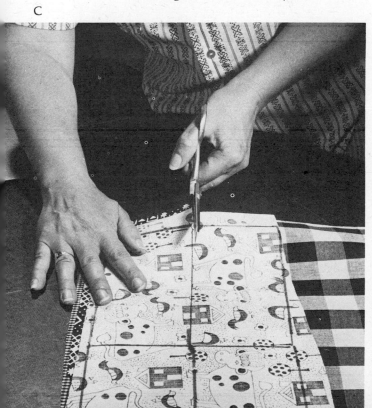

D

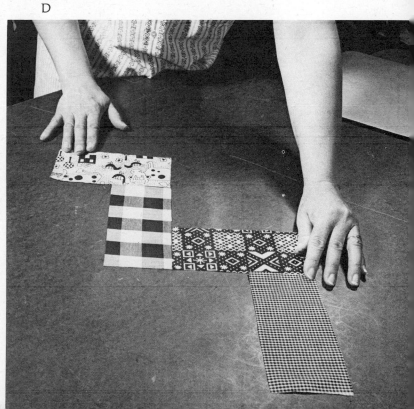

E. *Starting the second row of a block of Fence Rail.*
F. *A completed large block of Fence Rail.*

 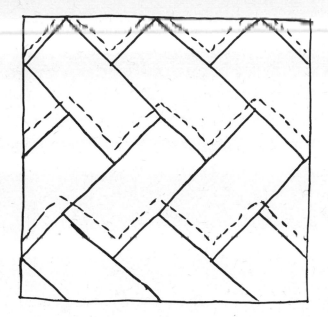

FIG. 42. *Fence Rail design and quilting pattern.*

After the entire quilt top is pieced, square it off by cutting away all the jagged points. Assemble with batting and backing in a quilting frame and quilt one-half inch from the seam as in the quilting pattern shown in figure 42. When this is completed, finish by binding in a complementary color.

Within this simple pattern, variations in design can be worked through fabrics and color. In figure 43, page 87, the pieces are linked randomly, and the overall look depends upon the crispness of the individual printed fabrics. In Plate VI, facing page 22, eight fabrics are used. An alternation of four per line is used, and the order is strictly maintained. In every other line, two solid fabrics are used in exactly the same place to give a chevron stripe to the completed cover.

If one wants solid tooth-edged stripes, the same fabrics can be used in the same position in every line.

As one goes along with the quilting craft, its flexibility and the playful variations possible become more and more obvious. There's beauty in the old ways and beauty in accepting the challenge of adapting them to modern tastes.

Sharon Rockefeller was very fond of the Fence Rail quilts. During that summer, she was expecting her first child, but this did not prevent her from continuing her work with the Artisans. One might

Fence Rail variation.

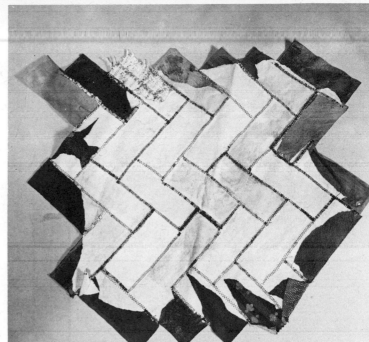

A   B

FIG. 43. *Fence Rail variation.*
  A. *Block of Fence Rail made of animal hides, simulated leathers, fake furs, and up-holstery fabrics. Because they are too heavy to be easily seamed, the blocks are pieced by machine zigzagging to a paper backing. In cutting pieces, do not add a seam allowance.*
  B. *View of the reverse side of the animal hide Fence Rail zigzagged to paper backing. After the block is completed, the paper is torn away.*

almost say that the organization and she were going through parallel pregnancies and, in addition to preparing for the birth of her own baby, she was among those playing midwife to the cooperative.

One afternoon she was visiting the office, and Dorothy suggested that it might be fun if the group made a quilt for the baby. Sharon agreed and commissioned them to make one using gay nursery colors in the Fence Rail pattern.

Dorothy thought it would make a pretty little quilt, but that it was hardly challenging as a design project. The others felt that they would like to do something special for young Mrs. Rockefeller, something memorable, something much more than merely a pretty little quilt. Not only were they all grateful to her for her help, but they genuinely liked and admired both of the Rockefellers, who, having the choice of lives of pleasant and luxurious idleness, had opted for dedication to public service.

Yes, something special was definitely in order. Fence Rails were not for the child of a couple who refused to be fenced in by traditions. "Something living! Animals!" Dorothy exclaimed. "I'll do some sketches of what I mean. They can be appliquéd in blocks, and the blocks pieced together."

Dorothy sketched what was originally conceived as an animal quilt but expanded to include flowers, and fish, and even adaptations of old Pennsylvania Dutch hex signs to ward off evil spirits. Her imagination was given free reign to abstract the forms and reassemble them into a child's wonderland of fanciful impressions (see fig. 44 page 88).

Originally she did six large blocks and a rough layout. But it was as if she had opened the door to the march of a magical menagerie. She could not stop the parade. Ideas kept springing at her. By the time she was finished, there were twenty blocks. What had been planned as the spread for a single bed had grown into an impressive wall hanging of sizable dimensions.

The drawings delighted everybody, but how were the marvelously drawn details to be translated into materials? This would obviously take more than simple appliqué. It would be an experiment in layering fabrics.

First, patterns of the largest shapes would be cut. These would be appliquéd to the blocks. Layer after layer, increasingly smaller pieces would be appliquéd. In some instances the process would be reversed. A top layer would be partially cut away to reveal the fabric beneath it. The very finest of the sketch lines would be rendered in embroidery.

FIG. 44. *Block designs for the Rockefeller quilt.*

Dorothy met with the groups in Lincoln County and explained what she wanted. They had never done or seen anything quite like it and were dubious to the point of suspecting that the designer was just a little bit crazy. But the sewing ladies were game. They were willing to try anything once.

Each block was given to a different woman. Just as there are variations in the depth, style, and skill of painters, so there are variations in the skill of quilters. This becomes apparent with a very careful examination of the individual blocks, but none of the women were less than capable and, when joined, all of the work blended into a beautifully executed entity. (See Plate VI facing page 22.)

The blocks were of varying shapes and sizes. Their final placement was like putting together a large jigsaw puzzle. While the women were working, all Dorothy had was a master key (see fig. 45 page 90) indicating where everything belonged. She had nightmares of losing it and never being able to figure out exactly how to put the pieces together.

The designer worked very closely with the crafters. "I kept reassuring them, telling them not to worry, saying I knew it was going to be okay. I pretended that I had great confidence. But I didn't really. I just had a vision and prayed. For the embroidery, all I did was give rough ideas. One of the great things about my relationship with the women is that often I just suggest that I'd like an outline stitch in a certain place, but if they get a little carried away that's all right, too. It's always worked out well. They've been satisfied, and I've been satisfied. They have a good bit of freedom within a framework. It's good. It gives them a sense of creative participation. The women tease me a lot—make jokes about Dorothy and her crazy ideas. But they really enjoy them. They enjoy the challenge of a change."

Starting with first design sketches, the execution of the Rockefeller quilt took from early June 1969 to mid-September 1970. But there were breaks to fill other orders and for vacations. If the work had been concentrated, the actual construction would have taken one group two or three weeks of full-time labor.

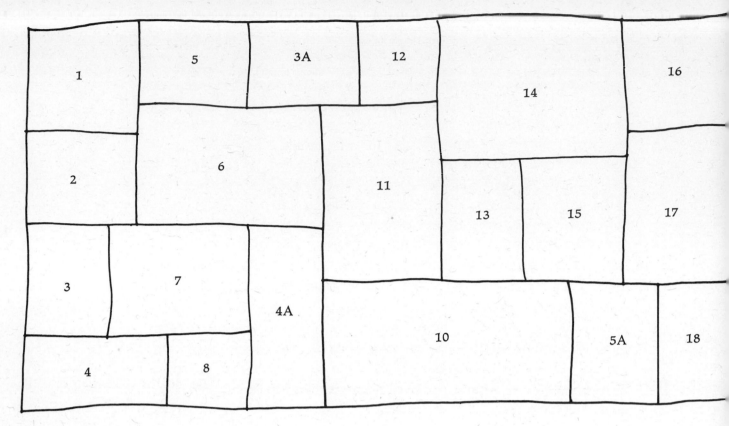

FIG. 45. *Rockefeller quilt layout.*

When the blocks were completed, they were turned over to the women of the Sod Sewing Group. Working under the supervision of Blanche Griffith, the Sewing Group pieced the blocks together, basted the completed top to the batting and backing, and did the actual quilting in a frame. The quilting was done unobtrusively in outlining stitches around the figures and shapes in the designs.

There was a rush at the end to complete the work in time for an open house tour of the Rockefeller home, so that the new quilt could be a focal point, demonstrating the brilliant craftsmanship of the Mountain Artisans.

Working full time, it took five Sod women two days to do the job. Dorothy Weatherford will never forget the day that they actually finished.

"I drove out to pick it up early, on a hot September afternoon. When I got there, the women were all grinning, as they spread it out before me. I'd never before seen it all put together. I'd only seen blocks. It was like seeing a whole new thing. I thought—did I really design that? I still react that way to many of the things. I put them down on paper and select fabrics, then they're all taken away to be processed and made. And I don't see them again until they're all finished. You'd be surprised at how often I'm surprised that they really work."

The Rockefeller quilt did, indeed, work. It represents the Mountain Artisans at the peak of their excellence. Many critics consider it a masterpiece of design and quilting. It has been loaned for craft exhibits all over the country. There is no doubt that it is one of those rare examples of craft becoming fine art.

When a group could turn out a piece of work of such extraordinary quality so early in its history, the potential was phenomenal. The future was a thing of boundless promise. The only problem was persevering until it was fulfilled. The summer of the Rockefeller quilt was the first of their existence. The question of a second was in such doubt that they considered each day passed a day gained.

Despite the quality, the dedication, the New York interest, the orders, and the loan, reaching sunset was still exhaustingly problematic at dawn.

The Artisans had a staff, but they had to invent their organization as they went along. The only thing they really knew was how to avoid the mistakes of others who had tried cooperative enterprises before them. Beyond that, for all their idealism, how long would it be possible to keep this competent group together without any promise of salaries? They had four excellent sewing groups, but how long could they be expected to hold themselves in readiness to fill orders, when there was so little continuity in work?

The problem was twofold—organization and finances. On the organizational level, they received a great boost when Claudia Schechter joined in the spring. Another tremendous asset was added when Claudia introduced another VISTA veteran, Rita Bank, into the group in the middle of that summer.

Rita started by volunteering to be a secretary. She freely admits that she was the world's worst secretary, but a secretary was what the group needed, and a secretary was what she became, despite the fact that her typing was not much better than her shorthand, which was nonexistent.

It was not long before a real managerial talent surfaced. The place was cluttered with idealists. In order for them to be free to dedicate themselves to their ideals, they needed somebody else to do the bookkeeping, see that the bills were paid, merchandise shipped, and invoices sent. Rita became that somebody else and was given the title of office manager.

This is not to imply that Mrs. Bank was short on idealism herself. She really believed in the cooperative system, especially when tinted with a shade of Women's Lib.

"I think that cooperatives give you a chance to have some sort of meaningful relationship to production. When somebody works her butt off all day long, then she's the one who should get something back from a business when it makes money. Now, of course, that only refers to production cooperatives. I also believe in service cooperatives like supermarkets. You invest money and split up profits according to how much food you've bought. It makes a lot of sense.

"Another exciting thing about working for Mountain Artisans is that the place is all women. The look on a man's face, when he walks in for the first time and is going to do business with us—it's worth all of the pains we've had. It's just incredible. The same thing when you speak to a man on the phone, and he says—let me talk to your boss. And you say—I'm my boss.

"A lot of men are quite obnoxious about it. They think of—well—loving hands at home, a lot of women down there working in sewing bees. They don't understand, it's a real business, and the women who do the sewing know a lot about it. Then, they come down here. And it's a revelation to them. It's incredible how backward men are about these things."

Rita was not unique. It was a crazy combination of belief in the Mountain Artisans and the ability to do a job that inspired each of the early movers—Florette, Dorothy, Claudia, and Rita.

The Office of Economic Opportunity would undoubtedly mean salvation for them all but, though it looked as if they would get it, the grant would not be forthcoming by the time they needed it—which was approximately the day before yesterday. In the meantime, the Artisans had practically reached the point of annihilation.

To survive, they made anything anybody asked for—placemats, tote bags, stuffed toys, even bedroom slippers. Most of the items subsequently became standard in their line. However, the bedroom slippers were never again repeated. They were handsome, but there was one small problem. The women were never able to turn out a pair with two of the same size. Astonishingly, some actually sold, giving Dorothy and Florette visions of rather strangely built people.

Summer became autumn amid a melange of crisis meetings that centered on the hope that they might be on the verge of something better than mere survival. All of Charleston's prominent business people gave them advice and support. Nobody gave them money.

Dorothy had designed a sensational line, but the women did not know if they should take the gamble on making the samples. Toward the middle of September, they began to get the first hints that the OEO was going to pick them up. On the strength of that, it was decided to go ahead with plans to return to New York with the new collection.

There remained the old problem. How were they to finance production? Florette returned to Bill Shearer, at the Kanawha Bank and Trust. His initial reaction to the request for a second loan of $7,000, before repayment of the first, was a baleful "Oh, God!"

Fortunately, this was followed by an almost inaudible whisper, "I can't let you down now."

Shearer was probably the first banker in history to have succeeded in turning a Trust Company into an In-God-We-Trust Company.

By their second collection, the Mountain Artisans had already

FIG. 46. *Tumbling Blocks quilt.*

94

established a definite look for all of their collections to come. It was a blend of Dorothy's exciting new designs and her adaptations of traditional patterns like Tumbling Blocks (see fig. 46 page 94), done in bright colors and new fabrics.

Tumbling Blocks is an optical illusion pattern that looks much more difficult to make than it really is. To make it, first draw the pattern, using a heavy paper or cardboard and follow the instructions in figure 47. Cut the three pieces. Then follow the instructions on pages 96–97, figure 48.

When the entire quilt is assembled, square the edges, assemble with batting and backing, and quilt according to the quilting pattern in figure 49. Quilt ½" from seams. After the quilting is completed, bind the quilt in a complementary color.

Late in September, just before departing for New York, the Mountain Artisans were informed that they had been given the OEO grant. They were awarded $189,000 for that year, with the indication that it would be a continuing grant for every year that they needed it.

Along with the grant, they had to take on some sewing groups that had been operating under another OEO project, the Coopera-

FIG. 47. *Making pattern pieces for the Tumbling Blocks quilt. Measure off a 20" square. Fold in half, lengthwise, then in half across the width and in half again (dotted lines in drawing). Using a ruler, connect the folds according to the heavy lines in the drawing. Cut along the connecting lines and keep the three pattern pieces, marked A, B, and C. Retrace each pattern on a separate piece of paper and add ⅜" seam allowance around the sides of each piece. With these pieces cut the fabric to make the pattern.*

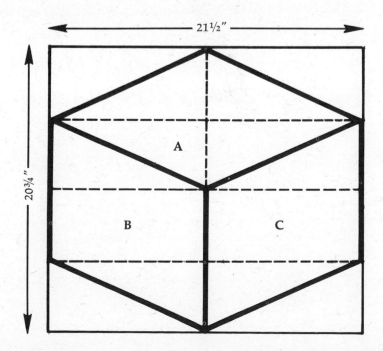

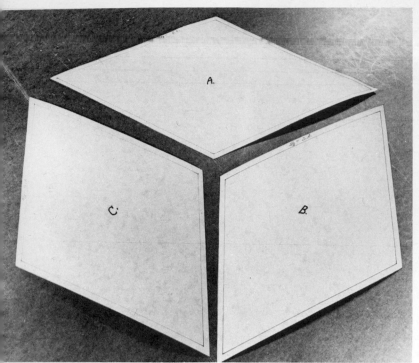

A   B

Fig. 48. *Making the Tumbling Blocks quilt.*

A. *The three pattern pieces for Tumbling Blocks. Assembled, they represent one block. To determine the number of blocks necessary for a quilt, divide 20 into the number of inches of width and of length. Multiply the results. For example, a quilt 120" by 100" would take 30 blocks. Note that every other row uses half-blocks on the ends.*

B. *Select the fabrics. This pattern works best with specific color placement. The same fabric should be used consistently for each pattern piece. The most effective block use has the top block piece (A) in a dark color, and the under pieces (B and C) in light colors. Pin the pattern to the appropriate fabric and cut.*

C. *Assembling the pieces for one block.*

D

D. Adding the second block.
E. A Tumbling Block using very tailored prints.

E

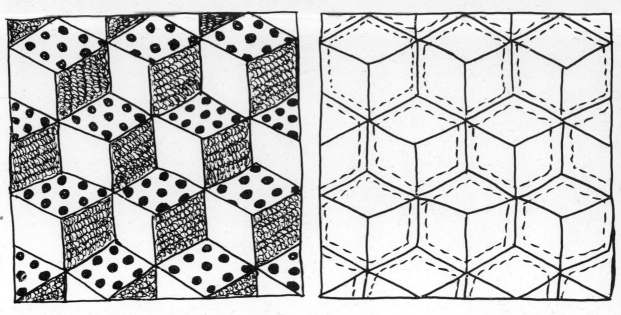

FIG. 49. *Giant Tumbling Blocks design and quilting pattern.*

tive Business Development Program. The CBDP actually had been started to generate jobs for men. Although it did a fairly good job with the women, it was not really oriented to dealing with the specific problems of these groups. Consequently, they were not being utilized to their own, or anybody else's, full advantage. The OEO felt they would do much better under the aegis of the Mountain Artisans, which was showing every indication of becoming expert in handling the quilting craft.

As the new groups contained very adept needle-women, they proved a great asset to the Artisans. But the grant was not an unmixed blessing. The money could not be used to pay the groups for their labor, nor could it be used for the purchase of materials. It could only be used for expenses, overhead, and the development of new work.

For the grant to be meaningful, they had to get enough orders to keep the groups in production. In other words, the selling trip had to produce far more significant results than the $7,000 garnered during the first excursion.

The first week in New York was utter disaster. There was still some sales resistance based on the bad CBDP experience. Although some items were priced as low as $20, others ranged to $700, and everybody was telling them that they were too expensive. But there was no way to bring costs down. In order to pay for the hand labor, the cooperative had to sell what they produced in the better market. (They were also still buying much of their fabric in retail stores.)

Dorothy was ready to quit and left for home in utter dejection. The only way to cut costs was to increase volume. The only way to increase volume was to get large orders at the high prices. It seemed hopeless, a circle that led them right back to where they had started.

Nevertheless, there had to be a solution. The enormous enthusiasm for what they were doing was still in evidence. They were still the darlings of the fashion magazines, but their stories would hit the stands too late to do any good. They needed immediate exposure in the market. Fortunately, they got it.

Women's Wear Daily, the powerful trade paper of the feminine apparel industry, came to do a story during that dismal first week. *WWD* has made and ruined more big fashion names than any other publication in the world. When a fantastically laudatory piece on the Artisans appeared during their second week in New York, the tide turned. There was no longer any consideration of pricing: when riding the crest, the tide is never too high. *WWD* had made another reputation.

Using the skills of their ancestors in a new way, the women of the West Virginia hills—who had never heard of the fashion centers of Seventh Avenue and Avenue Mantignon—had helped to bring about a minor revolution in style that added a new dimension to the way women dressed. Skirts like Dresden Plate, employing a traditional quilting pattern, became the "in" look (see fig. 50 page 100).

The response to the second New York showing proved conclusively that the Artisans had been right to keep faith with their project. There was a large potential market for their wares, and, what was still more important to the survival of the project, they were beginning to find it. Orders had multiplied almost tenfold. They were definitely on their way.

Certainly a major portion of the credit belongs to Dorothy Weatherford. The staff was constantly both amazed and delighted

FIG. 50. *Dresden Plate skirt.*

by the facility with which she was able to turn her talents to the creation of new designs within a traditional framework. The basis for some of her patterns was as old as the quilting craft, but she was able to make them look different, to revitalize them by release from the conventions of the past.

She describes her approach this way:

> "I find no difference in my approach to designing quilted things and my approach to the so-called fine arts. For me, a cover becomes a canvas, and I think of it in terms of an exercise in two-dimensional composition. A skirt is three-dimensional, and my thoughts immediately turn to sculptural effects."

If one of the quilting women told her that what she wanted had never been done before, she asked—why not? The answer was often because the materials were either unavailable or too expensive. Quilting in the hills had always been a way of utilizing serviceable scraps of materials from old clothes and bedding. More recently, remnants from fabric discount stores have become available at very low prices.

The Mountain Artisans had no remnants nor could they have used them for their merchandise. They had to buy in bulk in order to produce in bulk. They also had access to a great variety of materials available only to people in the trade. There was no reason for them to be enslaved to traditional cloths. Why not use bright, bold colors, the newer weaves, modern prints, fake or real furs, leather, suede? Why not use anything that could be pieced with needle and thread?

Once the women in the groups saw the possibilities, they began to look at their own work with a broader vision. The new fabrics were also accessible to them. All of the members of all of the groups could avail themselves of the sizable amount of scraps left over after the completion of a job for the Artisans. Nothing was ever discarded. A barrel was kept, and with an economy inherited from their ancestresses, the women saved every scrap in it and were free to help themselves when creating their own things.

A new look was coming into their homes via the new materials coupled with a fresh sense of what could be done with them.

Mrs. Pauline Bosley is the mother of nine children. Eight are girls, and they all live at home. She is a member of the Upsher County Sew & Sew Group, and the Artisans have furnished her with a new sewing machine to enable her to do her work at home. She laughed and said, "I made a spread for myself with scraps. I've got enough left to make matching drapes. It's very bright, but I find I like those bright colors. And for a change, my husband liked it. A lot of the time, he don't like the things I design and figure out. But he liked that. He was real proud of it."

She continued, "I like the Artisans' quilts. They look better than what our mothers and grandmothers made. They used to put so much white in them. I like the colors. They don't show the dirt as bad either."

She gazed around at her sizable young family and laughed fondly. "In this house, that's important." She became serious again. "Some of the things we do—one of the big quilts we made went to Mrs. Lawford, President Kennedy's sister, you know. Another to the Smithsonian Institute. It makes you feel good to make things like that. To know that people's really seeing them and buying them."

Dorothy's special look not only was influencing the style centers, but it was also changing the look of the homes of the people in the hills. Mrs. Bosley's sewing machine goes night and day, as she does her work for the group and her adolescent daughters take turns making things for themselves to wear modeled on the Weatherford designs that their mother executes.

The Dresden Plate skirt looks very lush and complicated but, as in all examples of the craft, it really is anything but difficult once the three basics of piecing, appliqué, and quilting are mastered. In this garment, all three are used. (See fig. 50 page 100.) To make the Dresden Plate skirt, twelve blocks are necessary. The six visible in the front view of the skirt (fig. 50) are duplicated in the rear.

To make the skirt, three cardboard patterns are necessary. A large rectangle, 12¾" by 15¾", will serve for cutting the blocks.

A circle with a diameter of 2¾" is needed for cutting the center of the flowers (1⅜" is the point on a compass).

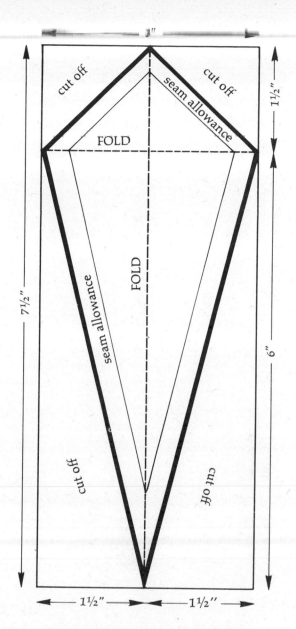

FIG. 51. *Dresden Plate petal pattern.*

For the petals of the flowers, see figure 51 on page 103. Draw a rectangle measuring 3″ by 7½″. Divide it in half lengthwise. 1½″ from the top, divide it across the width. With a ruler, link the tips of the dividing lines or folds. Cut. This will give the petal pattern, including a ⅜″ seam allowance which grows very long at the bottom point. Don't worry about that.

Purchase ½ yard each of four complementary solid-color fabrics (i.e. gold, orange, red, purple). Using the large rectangular pattern, cut three blocks from each fabric. Block placement and quilting plan

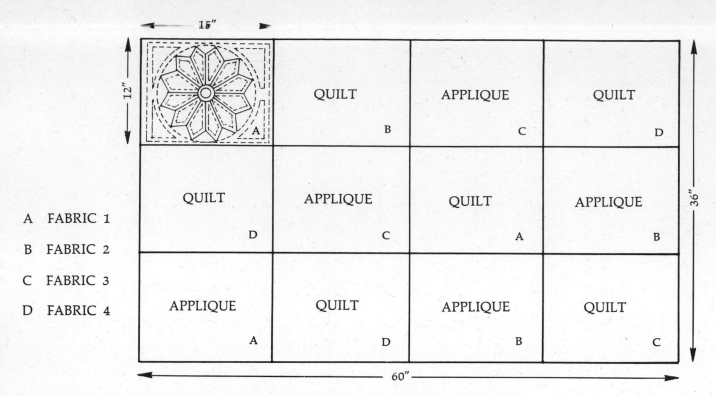

A	QUILT B	APPLIQUE C	QUILT D
QUILT D	APPLIQUE C	QUILT A	APPLIQUE B
APPLIQUE A	QUILT D	APPLIQUE B	QUILT C

A FABRIC 1
B FABRIC 2
C FABRIC 3
D FABRIC 4

FIG. 52. *Block placement and quilting pattern for Dresden Plate skirt.*

are shown in figure 52 page 104. Notice that the blocks are placed so that no two blocks of the same color ever touch. The quilting pattern remains the same for those with flower appliqués and those that are unadorned. Now follow the directions given in figure 53 on pages 105–113 for making the blocks for the Dresden Plate skirt.

Repeat the steps given in figure 53 until all the flowers are constructed and all but one are appliquéd. As indicated in figure 52, the appliqués go on two blocks each of Fabrics 1, 2, and 3. There are no appliqués on any of the blocks of Fabric 4. Take the reserved flower and lightly draw an outline of it in the centers of all the blocks of Fabric 4 and one block each of Fabrics 1, 2, and 3. This will serve as a guide in drawing the quilting pattern on those blocks without appliqués. Appliqué the last flower.

After piecing the blocks into a 36¾" by 60¾" rectangle, following the placement instructions in figure 52, select a 1½" ribbon of a complementary color (or of one of the block colors). Center it directly over all the seams connecting the blocks and hand appliqué it in place. A seam allowance is unnecessary.

A

B

FIG. 53. *Directions for making the blocks for the Dresden Plate skirt.*

A. *The necessities for making the petals for one flower. Scissors, the cardboard petal pattern, a marker, and six fabrics. Each flower has twelve petals—two cut from each of the different fabrics.*

B. *Outlining the petal pattern on the fabric.*

C. *Cutting the petals.*

D. *Half of the petals for one flower. The other half will be its exact duplicate, but petals of the same pattern will be placed opposite each other, so that the petal on the extreme left follows the one on the extreme right, then the one next to it, etc.*

Each of the six flowers in the skirt can be different, or they can all be the same. If the same fabrics are to be used, there is another method of cutting the petals (see illustrated steps E through G).

C

D

E

F

E. On a large piece of fabric, trace the pattern.

F. End on end, keep tracing as many as possible or necessary. A maximum would be 24 to cover two petals for each appliqué in the skirt.

G. Cutting the petals from a strip of fabric.

H. Tracing the circle pattern on a fabric for the centers of the flowers.

G

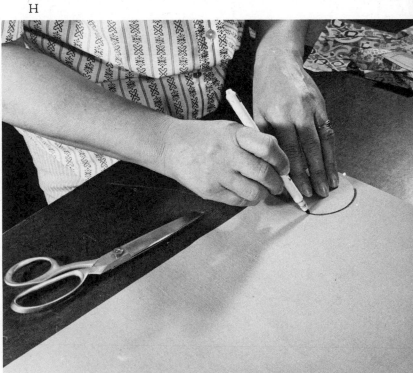

H

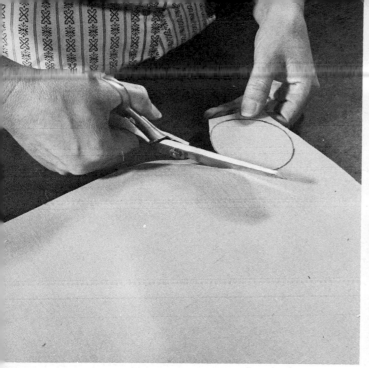

I   J

I. Cutting the center. Six of these are necessary; and they are all cut from the same fabric. This fabric should be complementary to the colors in the petals.

J. Half of the petals and the center of one flower laid out on the block.

K. Piecing the petals by machine. Notice that a ⅜" seam allowance is used.

K

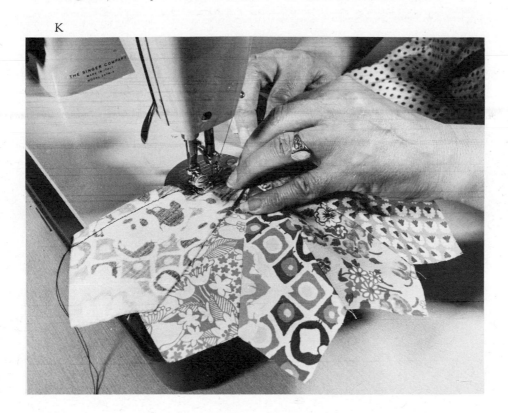

L. *Ready to piece the last petal to the flower.*

M

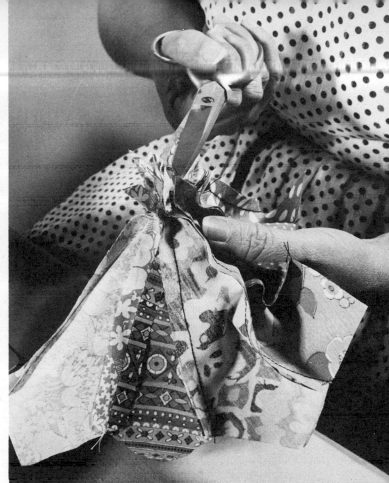

N

M. *Closing the first and last petals.*

N. *Snip away the excess seam allowance at the center of the pieced petals.*

O. *The completed petals ready for the next step. Seam allowances are trimmed and pressed down.*

P. *Place the flower center in the center of the petals and fold under the seam allowance.*

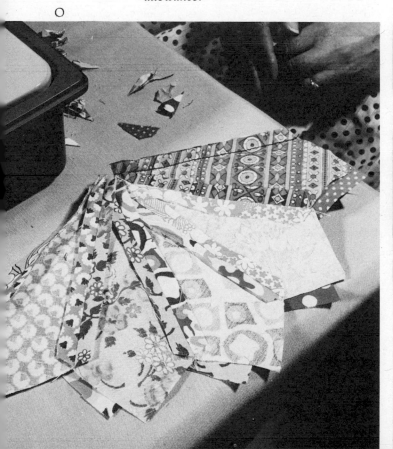

O

P

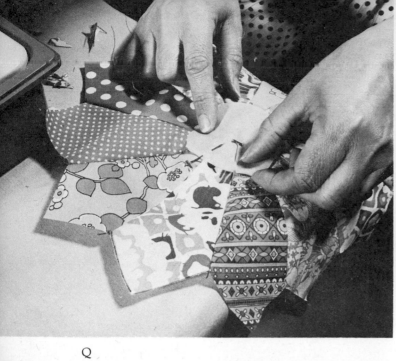

Q

R

Q. *Pin up the seam allowance and anchor it to the petals.*

R. *Appliqué the center to the petals.*

S. *Take the block to which the flower will be appliquéd and fold it in half.*

T. *Fold it in half again.*

S

T

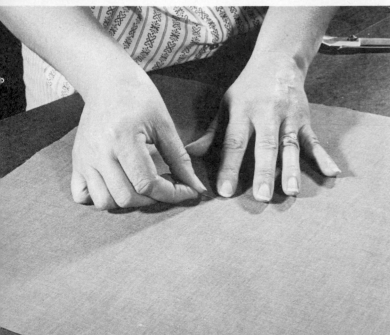

U. *Place a pin at the center of the block where the two folds intersect.*

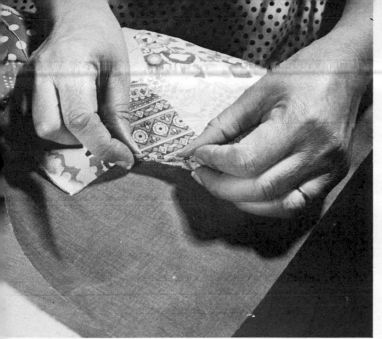
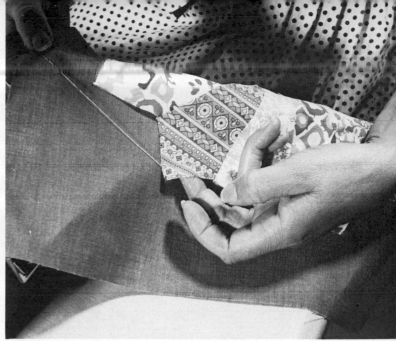

V

W

V. After pinning the center of the flower over the center of the block, start folding up the seam allowance at the end of one of the petals.

W. Start appliquéing the petal to the block. Repeat and continue until the entire flower is appliquéd.

X. The completed block with the center of the flower already quilted.

X

Y. *The quilting on one of the blocks without appliqué.*

Mark all the flower blocks with the quilting pattern in figure 52. Using the drawn outlines on the blank blocks as guides, sketch the quilting pattern on them.

Note: All drawing on finished blocks should be done very lightly in an erasable substance such as chalk.

Place skirt top, a layer of batting, and a thin backing (i.e. muslin) in a quilting frame or hoop.

On blocks with appliqués, quilt inside the petals of the flowers. On those without appliqué, quilt along the outlines of the petals (see step Y of fig. 53).

After quilting, remove from the hoop or frame and add one-inch strips of the same fabrics that are used in the blocks along the bottom of the wide end of the rectangle, until the width measures the desired length of the skirt plus a little extra to make a hem. Hand appliqué another row of ribbon over the seam connecting the bottoms of the blocks and the first strip of fabric.

Stitch up the center back seam and insert a zipper at the top.

Hand appliqué another row of ribbon over the back seam. Leave it open on one side over the zipper and attach snaps.

Gather into a proper size of waistband, also made from one of the fabrics used in the skirt blocks.

To make a Dresden Plate quilt or spread, simply keep adding rows of blocks, in the same scheme of alternation, until the desired size is reached. Bind in the same ribbon used to cover the seams.

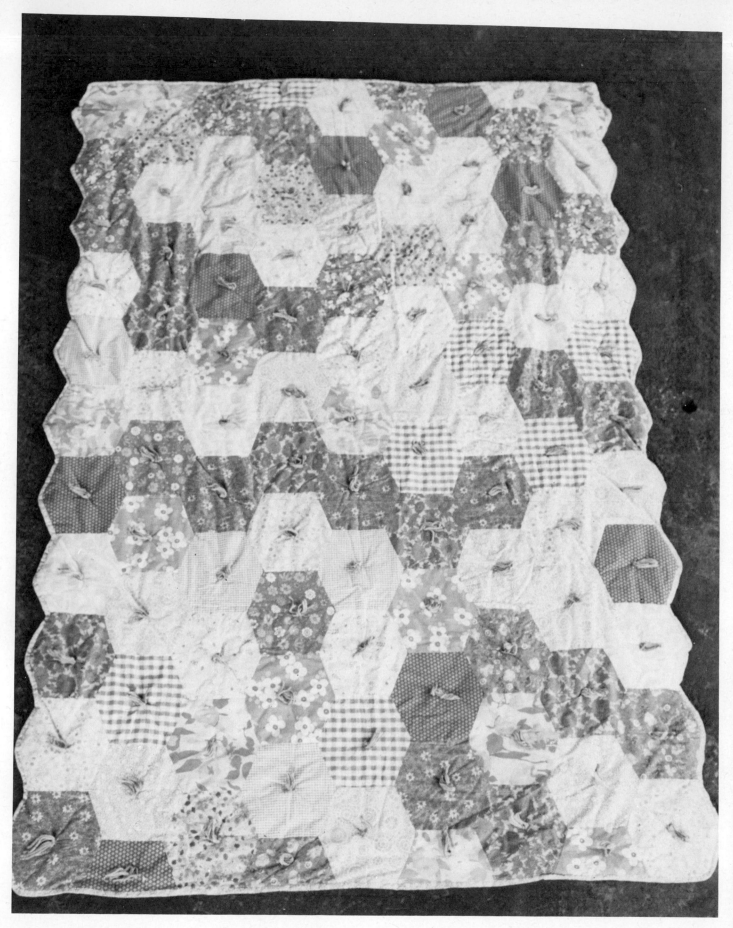

Giant Maxigon quilt.

CHAPTER SIX

"What with rearin' a family, and tendin' to a home, and all my chores—that quilt was a long time in the frame. The story of my life is pieced into it. All my joys and all my sorrows."

—Lincoln County quilter

O<small>NE</small> of the provisions for getting the Office of Economic Opportunity grant was that a majority of the board had to be made up of people rendering the service. This is a requirement in all government poverty and self-help projects. When the Mountain Artisans drew up new bylaws for submission to the OEO, they stated that 51 percent of the board members would be women from the sewing groups. It actually worked out that 60% come from the groups.

The necessary change was a very healthy one for the organization. It enabled them to get rid of some members who had been taking only a cursory interest and, more important, those who had displayed a lack of faith during the difficult summer.

In the beginning, there was some doubt about the effectiveness of sewing women sitting on a board. None of the Charleston people knew how it would work. Even the least faithful of the former members had belonged to committees and had been sitting on boards throughout most of their adult lives. They knew their rights as board members, knew what a board was supposed to do and how it functioned.

For the women from the hills and hollows, it would be a new and possibly intimidating experience. How would they react? Would they recognize their rights, or would they be overawed by the more verbal and experienced minority? Most of all, would they be a hindrance or a help?

In her capacity as field worker, Claudia Schechter had come to know the women very well. She had faith in their intelligence and in their ability to assume responsibilities. It was only a question of training them in the fundamentals of procedure, and she insisted upon the immediate institution of a training program. It continues to this day so that, by the time a woman gets on the board, she knows why she is there.

The mountain quilters were a different breed from their urban colleagues on the board. They were different from city people on almost every level. If it paid a wage, no job was too menial for them. They were proud of working. They were ashamed of any form of idleness.

The people in the hollows enjoyed working with their hands. The hills abounded with fine craftsmen. There was a delicacy, an artistry in their touch. It is a truth that any man who can carve or build, and any woman who can sew, or cook, or quilt, is creative.

It is a rare visitor to their homes who is not treated to a display of ancestral quilts. The hollows women are as proud of them as any city woman showing off grandma's silver. But there is an enormous difference. The mountain heirlooms are living and growing things. It is more than likely that a new quilt that will pass down the years from daughter to daughter is in the frame at the very moment that grandmother's coverlet is being spread before the caller.

If the visitor looks only at the modest homes and simple ways of the hills, he sees only the surface. He does not see the depth which can only be measured in time.

Time moves slowly in Appalachia. There are no abrasive changes of pace. The people are not subjected to the traumatic disorientation of speed. Cities do not spring up in a month. The country ways are not swept away in a frenzy of urbanization.

In the slowness of time, there is time for everything. Was it yesterday or a hundred years ago that this quilt was pieced? Does it matter? The quilt remains. The pattern is repeated in the quilt in the frame. It is still valid. It is still beautiful. It will give pleasure and warmth for another hundred years to come.

Even space is measured in time. Along the winding country roads, miles are not the gauge of the distances between places. If a stranger asks for directions, he will likely be told that one place is three hours from another.

The material is cut and set aside, while the woman attends to another task. For there is time. The rows are slowly pieced and put away. For there is time. The cover remains in the frame to be quilted another day. For there is time.

And patience is born of time, the patience to cut and count and piece the Roman Stripe quilt (see Plate VII facing page 23).

To make a Roman Stripe quilt, only one pattern is necessary. Follow the instructions in figure 54 on pages 118–119. After sewing together all the blocks and completing the quilt top, prepare it for the frame with batting and backing. Quilt with stitches ½ inch from the seams according to the pattern in figure 55. Bind with a complementary color.

Note: To make a Roman Stripe skirt, use a pattern piece measuring 6¾" by 2¼". This will give a 6" square block when pieced. Piece seven rows of twelve blocks each to make a rectangle measuring 42" by 72". Use the same construction as in making Sun Up skirt (fig. 27 pages 55–57). Make the waistband of the same fabric as one of the stripes.

One of the obstacles to creating a functioning quilting cooperative was the sense of timelessness in the hollows. Deadlines did not exist for most of the hill women, except those enforced by nature— seeds that had to be planted, cows that had to be milked and let out to pasture, vegetables that had to be canned. They did not worry about the exigencies of commercial deadlines, because they had never been in contact with them.

Early in its history, one of the southern groups calmly informed the Mountain Artisans home office that a batch of work that was due for delivery would not be finished in time. The miner's holidays were starting, and they were going off with their husbands on vacation. They told the office not to worry about it, that they would complete the work as soon as they returned. The information was forwarded on a postcard that did not arrive in Charleston until after they had all departed.

The incident was an isolated one and never again repeated. With the organization's systems of quality and production control, it could not happen today, but it is indicative of an early attitude toward time. This changed as the women, themselves, became aware

A

B

Fig. 54. *Instructions for making the Roman Stripe quilt.*

    A. *The basic materials for making a Roman Stripe block—cardboard or heavy paper pattern piece measuring 3¾" by 12¾" and four complementary fabrics.*

    B. *To make the pieces, layer the four fabrics and, using the cardboard or heavy paper rectangle, outline and cut the pattern exactly as in Fence Rail. (See fig. 41, B and C, on page 83.)*

    C. *To piece a block, simply stripe the four pieces of fabric. Subtracting seam allowance, this will give a 12" square. To calculate how many pieces of each fabric are necessary, divide 12 into the number of inches of width and length of the desired quilt and multiply the two results. After cutting, string the pieces, so that they won't get lost and the groups of each fabric can be kept separated. (See fig. 30 on page 63.)*

    D. *Place the blocks so that the stripes alternate going horizontally and then vertically.*

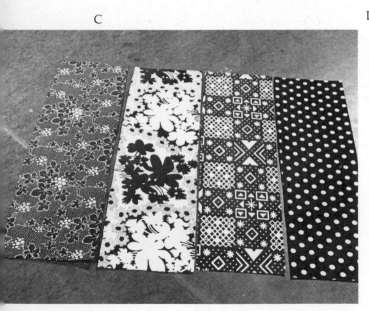

C

D

E. *Four blocks of Roman Stripe. Notice that the order of pieces remains the same in all blocks. The leafy print is followed by the bold floral, the geometric, and the polka dot. When this order is followed, the first stripe and last stripe form steps down the quilt.*

Fig. 55. *Roman Stripe design and quilting pattern*.

of the value of their work and of their importance to the success of the operation.

The male chauvinism of some of the mountaineers also occasionally led to early problems for the Artisans. The Upsher County Sew & Sew is run by Leona Underwood. It is the only group that works at home rather than meeting at a central point, and it is an extremely able one. But there were some initial obstacles that had to be overcome.

When Mrs. Underwood was first organizing the group, she found that many of the men did not want their wives to work. These husbands wanted to be the men of their houses in every way, even if it meant giving up some badly needed additional income. A woman took care of the home and children. A man provided the living.

There were homes where the husband would not remain in the room once Leona had entered. He thought that she did not have any business there. Hospitality is second nature to the people of the hills, and a man would never be so rude as to ask Leona to leave, but he made it clear that he would have preferred her not to be there.

While traditional family patterns are withering elsewhere, they remain very much alive in Appalachia. The people work too hard to question the values they labor to uphold. The deep familial commitment also works to the advantage of the Artisans. It has enabled them to pick up some excellent needle workers who could not have taken jobs with regular hours.

One of the Village Stitchery women commented, "I couldn't work full time. My husband wouldn't like it. I once had a steady job at the five and ten, but he didn't like it at all. Here, I can come in after he leaves for work, and I'm home before he gets home."

Another explained: "My husband passed away a year ago. I have three children in school. I've sewed and my mother before me. She made my clothes, and I make my daughter's. If it weren't for the kind of work with my own hours, I wouldn't have been able to go to work. I don't know what I'd have done. But my children come first. I think it's important to be there, when they get home. They had such a loss."

A third said, "I worked for six months at J. C. Penney. This is the first time I ever sewed for a living. Everybody here's so nice and cooperative. I have to work. My husband passed away, and I have to support myself. That's why I'm here. If I hadn't of come here, I'd have had to take a secretarial course or something—to get the training I need. So, this has been a wonderful help to me. It's neighborly work—neighbors doing for each other."

People do not die in the hills. They pass away. There is no abrupt alteration in the slowness of time, only a passing away that leaves behind those who are only capable of doing what they have always done—crafts, the domestic skills—and for these, especially, groups like the Mountain Artisans provide a means of survival with dignity.

The cooperatives have modernized the old quilting parties. There is still the sense of doing for each other, of women getting together, but there is also a sense of purpose and contemporary enterprise.

In areas of West Virginia, where any sort of commerce beyond the general store is rare, the women are learning how to operate a modern business by doing it themselves. Each group is responsible for its own expenses—rent, machines, wages—everything except the materials with which they work. They are not bound to the Mountain Artisans except by voluntary agreements. They are completely free to exercise their own designs for their own purposes. Their understanding with the organization is that they execute Artisans' designs at rates set by the specific group that made the original sample from the pattern based on Dorothy's design. The other groups either agree to live with that group's decision, or they reject the work.

Each group has a representative on the board of directors. Although they have constituted a majority since the OEO grant, it is only recently that they have been making themselves heard.

In addition to the large board there are small committees that deal with such specifics as finances, pricing, and loans to groups to buy new equipment. It was in these meetings that the women first started to offer their opinions. The groups were smaller and dealt with problems that related directly to them.

As the realization came that their opinions counted, they began to offer them more freely. The turning point was a self-regulatory resolution proposed and passed by the women. Being on the board represents an economic sacrifice to the individual members: on meeting days, they lose a full day's wages. The only payment they receive is compensation for the cost of transportation. Getting to and from Charleston is in itself often a hardship. For many of the women it means starting out at five or six in the morning and not getting home until after nine at night.

In the beginning, some members simply did not think it was worth the effort, and they did not show up for meeting after meeting. The faithful felt that the absentees were taking advantage of them. The ruling they proposed and passed stated that if a representative did not show up for three meetings in succession, her group lost all Mountain Artisans work for a month. Since its passage, there have been no more than two or three women missing at any given board meeting.

More and more, the women in the groups are taking the initiative and assuming responsibility for their own future. The new attitude represents more than a head start. It's a giant leap into a complicated world that, in a limited way, embraces modern approaches to technology and finance. And they're doing very well, thank you.

That the hills women have been able to make these strides comes as no surprise to the Charleston staff. One of the things that has drawn them to the work they are doing is the knowledge that there is an enormous difference between lack of opportunity and lack of ability to cope with it should it come along.

Virgie Riffle is just one example of the innate capacities of these women. Virgie posed for and did all of the sewing, cutting, and construction in the craft photographs in this book. She first joined Mountain Artisans as a seamstress in the Village Stitchery sewing group. It was not long before she was managing that group. When she moved to Charleston, she became a member of the staff of the home office and was put in charge of quality control. She was recently made Field Supervisor, which makes her the liaison officer between the groups and the home office in charge of all field operations and responsible for the training of all newcomers.

For generations, the Appalachians have been improvising on limited resources, developing handcrafts, using their native skills to improve the quality of their lives. The tremendous chic of the appliquéd dress in Plate XVI, facing page 150, is the result of a sophistication of craft that is indeed dazzling.

As the Mountain Artisans has grown, the women have expanded their skills. The greater the volume of work that they have handled, the better the quality. It is not a case of practice making perfect—that is a fallacious cliché—but of practice leading to a perfecting process, a refinement of technique.

The new quilter will discover this firsthand. The more work done, the better the quilting will become. Although the first quilting steps might seem formidable, once they are taken, the novice will find a rich reward and soon start to sense a growth in adeptness. There will be a desire to strike out in new directions, such as designing new patterns or improvising on old ones. It is improvisation that is the first step from homemade to handmade. One of Dorothy Weatherford's most rewarding experiences as a designer has been the feedback of viable new ideas from the creative quilters of the West Virginia hills.

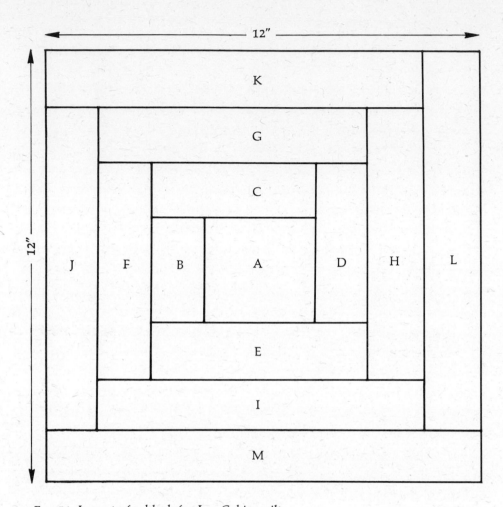

FIG. 56. *Layout of a block for Log Cabin quilt.*

Color is an important part of the new look in quilts. Dorothy is constantly experimenting with the potential for change that can be made simply by the juxtaposition of shades.

Log Cabin is a late eighteenth-century pattern. When executed only in vivid black and white prints, it takes on an abstract and very contemporary look.

The Log Cabin block is a 12″ square (see fig. 56 for quilt block layout). To make it, thirteen cardboard pattern pieces are necessary. Designating them by letter and in order of placement for piecing, measure and cut:

A. 3¾" by 3¾"   G. 8¼" by 2¼"
B. 3¾" by 2¼"   H. 8¼" by 2¼"
C. 5¼" by 2¼"   I. 9¾" by 2¼"
D. 5¼" by 2¼"   J. 9¾" by 2¼"
E. 6¾" by 2¼"   K. 11¼" by 2½"
F. 6¾" by 2¼"   L. 11¼" by 2½"

M. 12¾" by 2¼"

All of these include a ⅜" seam allowance.

Dimensions for this quilt should be in multiples of 12". Determine the number of blocks needed by dividing 12 into both the length and the width and then multiplying the two results. This last figure will also give the number of pieces of each letter that will be used. Cut and piece according to the instructions in figure 57 on pages 126–129.

After the quilt top is completed, assemble with batting and backing and place in a frame and quilt according to the pattern in figure 58. Bind in a complementary color and finish.

Log Cabin lends itself to many variations. It all depends on the juxtaposition of light and dark colors in the thirteen patterns used. In Plate VIII, facing page 23, shades of orange, red, green, and blue are used, and they are grouped according to color. Pieces A, B, F, and J are orange. Pieces D, H, and L are blue. Pieces C, G, and K are green. Pieces E, I, and M are red. After piecing, to achieve this particular play of dark and light, blocks are connected so that M is on the bottom, right side, bottom, etc., across the first row. In the second row, M is on the right side, bottom, etc., across, and placement is alternated in this manner all the way down the quilt.

There are other variations. For the spiralling effect, two to four colors in thirteen fabrics are utilized in values of intensity shown in illustration 59, page 130.

For the Windmill, any number of colors can be used as long as piece M is on the bottom then left side across the first row and on the right then top across the second—and repeated in this fashion down the cover.

Another way of doing Log Cabin has all the dark colors on one side, pieces B, C, F, G, J, and K, and all of the light colors on the other, pieces A, D, E, H, I, L, and M (see figs. 61 and 62 pages 131 and 132).

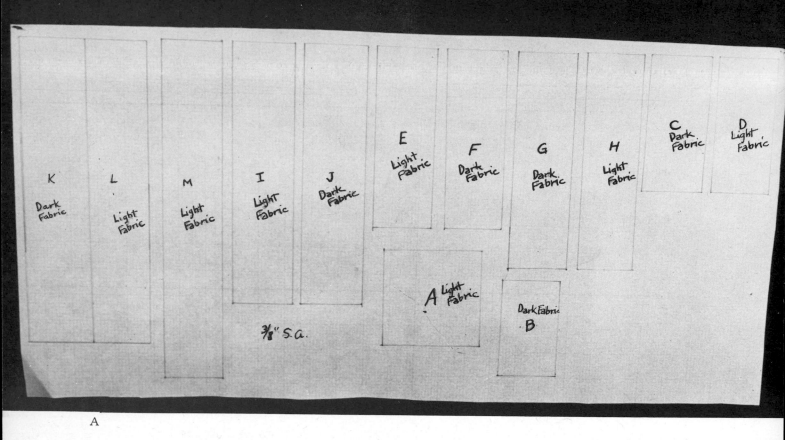

A

FIG. 57. Piecing Log Cabin block.

    A. *The thirteen Log Cabin pattern pieces before cutting. To avoid mistakes, always letter the pieces and indicate the color intensity (light or dark) right on the cardboard pieces. Outline the pattern on the fabric exactly as in Fence Rail (fig. 41, B and C, page 83), only in this case, the fabric is not layered. Each piece is cut from a different fabric. There are thirteen fabrics, one for each pattern piece.*

    B. *Laying out a block. A is always in the center. If B is on top, C is to the right.*

    C. *When C is to the right, D is placed below.*

B

C

D

E

D. When D is below, E is to the left.

E. Completing the layout of a block. In this, A is in the center. B is to its right; C is below; D to the left of A; E above; F to the right of B; G beneath C; H to the left of D; I above E; J to the right F; K beneath G; L to the left of H on the left-hand outside border. And M is in the process of being laid down above I (see fig. 56).

F. The actual piecing of the blocks can be done on a machine. To make life easy, always keep a plan of the piecing in front of you and string and mark each of 13 sets of pieces.

G. Piece B attached to piece A.

F

G

H

I

H. Blocks can also be pieced by hand.

I. Pieces A, B, and C joined. The block begins to take shape.

J. This is the back of figure 57 (I). Notice that in this picture A and B are machine
sewn and C is sewn by hand to show that both methods work.

J

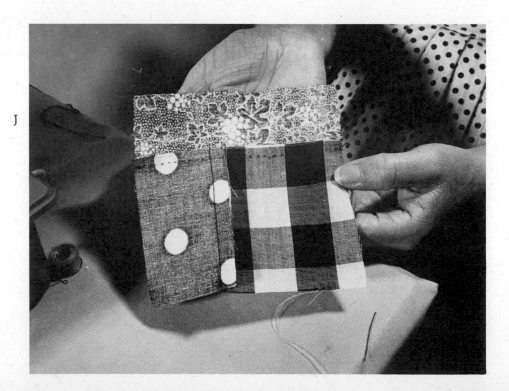

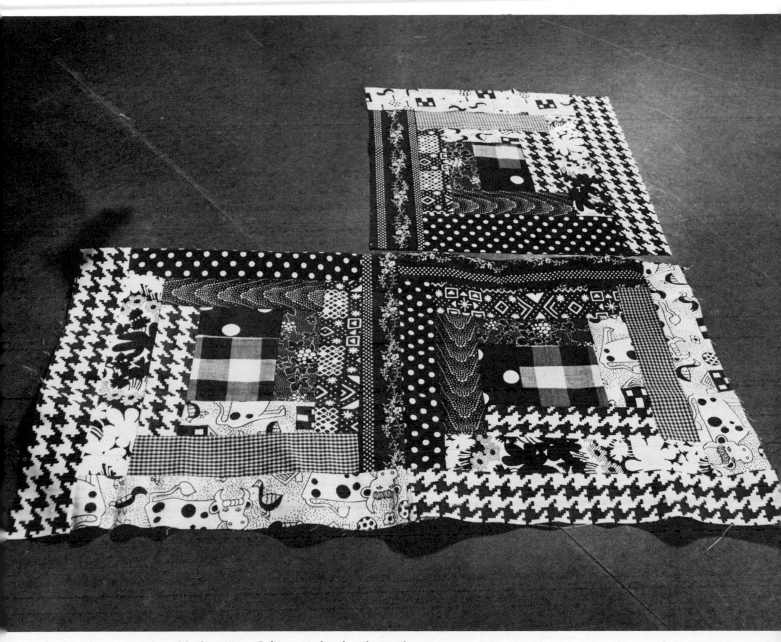

K. *Three blocks of Log Cabin completed and pieced.*

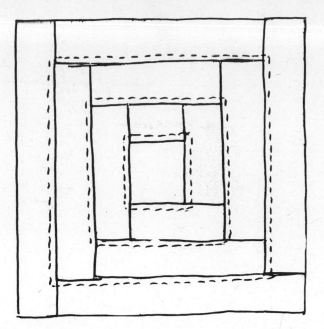

FIG. 58. *Quilting pattern for Log Cabin.*

FIG. 59. *Log Cabin block (spiralling effect).*

FIG. 60. *Log Cabin blocks (windmill effect).*

FIG. 61. *Log Cabin quilt (variation by juxtaposition of dark and light colors).*

FIG. 62. *Log Cabin block (variation by juxtaposition of light antd dark colors).*

In laying out traditional quilts, the designer can be so carried away by the brilliance of color, pattern, and texture available in materials that flights of fancy can transform them into entirely new things. The sheer richness of the fabrics can inspire one to make a Crazy quilt that is really only one enormous block as in the one shown in Plate XV, facing page 135. Patterns can cause the same sort of release, as with the animal prints in one of the quilts shown in Plate XV.

Touch fabrics, place them side by side, scatter them, layer them. Let the richness and variety open up the imagination. Once the three basics are learned, the possibilities of quilting can be endless.

In Plate IX, between pages 62 and 63, Dorothy allowed the placement, subtle toning, and juxtaposition of strips of leather, suede, and rough wools to determine the entire look of the quilt. Once one is freed from the old way of looking at things, there is no telling where the inspiration for a quilt may suddenly arise. Dorothy thinks it might even be in the doodling she idly does whenever a pencil and some paper are near. That's why she never throws anything away. She says, "I believe in doodling. I believe in any sort of subconscious creative release."

She also believes that everybody is capable of it and indulges in it. It takes no artistic training or talent. Even people with no esthetic orientation will doodle at odd moments and come up with fascinating combinations of shapes. Look at a housewife's shopping list or the pads around a conference table after a business meeting, or a piece of paper that happens to be near the telephone table.

It's almost as if the mind hungers for an artistic outlet to balance the mundane chores of day-to-day living. Inside every practical down-to-earth person there is a wild artist longing to get out. Quilting can provide a challenging and productive exit.

The budding designer should think of translating her doodles into blocks that might serve as the pattern for piecing (see fig. 63 page 133). Another approach to the transition from rough sketch to quilt is to use it as the source for the expansion of traditional patterns (fig. 64 page 134).

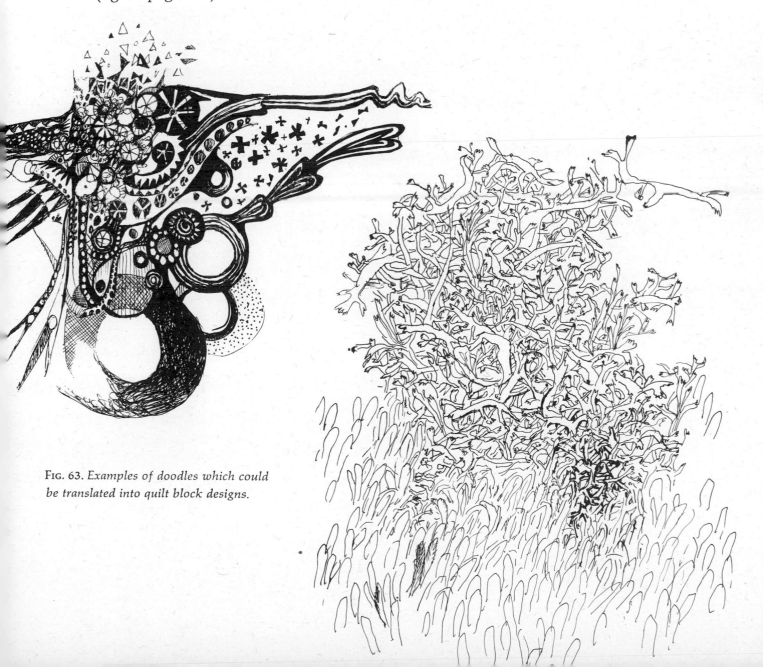

FIG. 63. *Examples of doodles which could be translated into quilt block designs.*

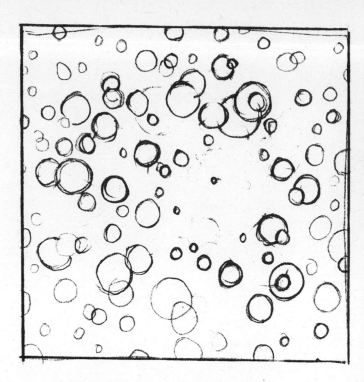

FIG. 64. *Rough sketches for the expansion of traditional patterns.*

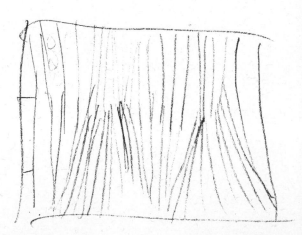

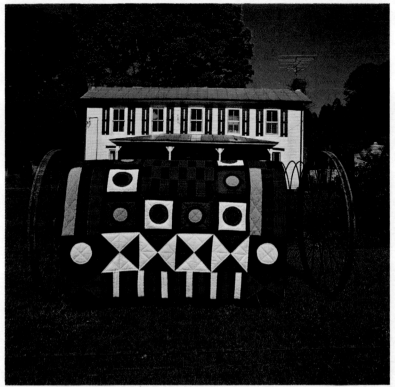

PLATE XII. *Geometric #1 quilt.*

PLATE XIII. *Floral Bouquet skirt.*

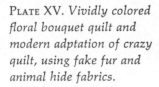

Plate XIV. *Floral Bouquet quilt.*

Plate XV. *Vividly colored floral bouquet quilt and modern adptation of crazy quilt, using fake fur and animal hide fabrics.*

In attempting one's own original designs—and Dorothy Weatherford believes that every quilter should eventually try her hand at creating and executing her own patterns—there are some fundamentals that should be borne in mind. The most important is that there are repetitions in every pattern, even a Crazy quilt. An overall quilt pattern emerges from the individual block patterns; something that might be quite bland by itself can glow vibrantly when repeated several times.

Repositioning blocks in relationship to each other can also change the total look. Altering colors from block to block, plays of dark and light coloring, textures—these are other ways of changing the total quilt by variations in parts.

To start, one might pursue a shape to discover the differences that can be worked by repeating it, reversing it, or dividing it. Zigzagging lines and angles can form a new adaptation of an old pieced block pattern. Can you see the relationship between the traditional Log Cabin, which has just been discussed, and the adaptation of it (fig. 65 page 136)? Even that adaptation becomes a springboard to something entirely new (fig. 66 page 136).

One can use the same types of angles and lines for a formal pattern (fig. 67 page 137) or a Crazy quilt (fig. 68 page 137).

In quilting, the simplest block of pieced right-angle triangles can be built into the most intricate of covers. The sketched block in figure 69 on page 137 is made up of eight triangles. There are five dark ones and three light ones. Two of the latter are cut in half, giving one large and four small light triangles.

Combine four of these original blocks to make one larger block with all of the arrowlike triangles pointing to the center (fig. 70 page 137). In this, another variation has been worked by substituting two triangles of different color or texture for two dark ones in both the upper right and lower left small blocks. Notice how an entirely new pattern has emerged by piecing the smaller pattern blocks.

To translate this into a cover, the next step would be to lay it out on graph paper doing six large blocks or a total of twenty-four smaller blocks. In figure 71 on page 138, a third pattern has developed from the piecing of the larger blocks.

FIG. 65. *Adaptation of Log Cabin design.*

FIG. 66. *Log Cabin design (markedly varied).*

136

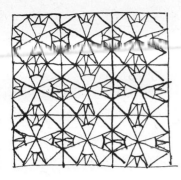

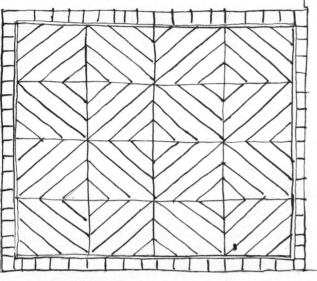

FIG. 67. Formal designs.

FIG. 68. Crazy quilt designs.

FIG. 69. Quilt block using pieced right-angle triangles.

FIG. 70. Large block made by combining quilt blocks like the one shown in figure 69.

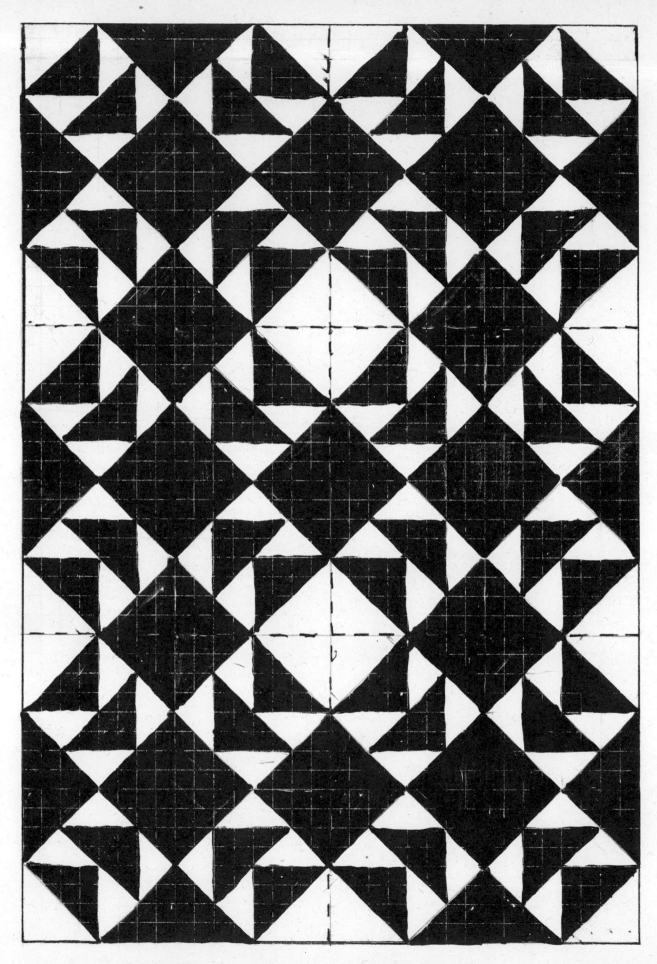

FIG. 71. *Pattern formed by combining large blocks like the one shown in figure 70.*

Graph paper is used in order to determine the exact size of a quilt finished to these specifications. If each space in the graph drawing represents two inches, the entire quilt measures 64″ by 96″.

The basic element is a triangle. By counting spaces it is found that the triangle has 8″ arms. To make the cardboard cutting pattern, draw a right-angle triangle with an 8″ side and add a ⅜″ seam allowance on all sides. For the smaller light triangles, simply cut the larger light triangles in half after they have been cut from the fabric.

The quilt can be enlarged by adding 16″ smaller blocks or 32″ larger blocks for as many rows top and bottom as are necessary. For example, the best way to make a king-sized spread measuring 120″ square would be to add one large and one small block to the width, one large block to the length, and finishing with an 8″ border of one of the colors in the quilt all around.

For this cover, the quilter could use solid colors, a combination of solids and prints, or all prints. She could also use suedes and leathers and fabrics in any combination she fancied. Colors and textures all change the look of the quilt. Another variation could be worked by reversing the tonal values and using dark fabrics where light are indicated and vice versa.

Placement changes the result. Pointing the arrowlike triangles away from the centers of the large blocks instead of toward them provides still another change in total design.

Once the particular direction has been decided and the top completed, lay it out with batting and backing and put in a quilting frame. See figure 72, page 140 for the quilting pattern. The running stitches should be ½″ inside the edge of the triangles.

If a border is used, repeat the triangle motif in quilting. (See fig. 73 page 140.)

It should be crystal clear that, starting with a simple shape like a triangle, one can easily evolve the most astonishingly complex quilt. The whole secret of designing for oneself is to start with a simple form and let oneself go.

FIG. 72. *Quilting pattern for large right-angle triangle blocks (follow broken lines).*

FIG. 73. *Border quilting pattern repeating triangle motif.*

Spinning Wheel is one of Dorothy Weatherford's most striking creations (see Plate XI, between pages 62 and 63). It measures 70″ by 110″ and hangs as a tapestry on the wall of the master bedroom of the Hatfield house, one of Charleston's most beautifully designed modern homes. The room has large windows overlooking the Kanawha River valley, and the hanging seems to be an abstraction of the view echoing all of the sharp, clean colors to be found in nature. The hues of the painted furniture, the bedspread, and the carpeting are keyed to the tones in the hanging.

As complicated as Spinning Wheel looks, it really is no more than a grand-scale employment of the three basics of piecing, appliqué, and quilting. In design, it is a lovely employment of two shapes—circle and rectangle.

The piece started with Dorothy's pursuit of the circle. She often experiments with one shape, exhausting all of its possibilities before turning to another, which might be followed by a return to the first. When she thinks she has gone as far as she can, the change will refresh her creative insights, and the return may well bring forth ideas that originally had not occurred to her.

At first, she merely broke up a square block with traditional patterns of a pinwheel and target (see fig. 74 page 141). It was not long before she put aside the target and started to concentrate on the pinwheel (see fig. 75 page 142).

FIG. 74. *Early target designs for Spinning Wheel.*

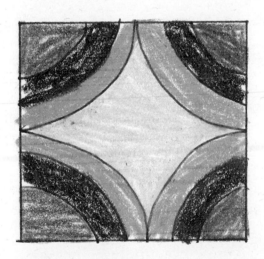
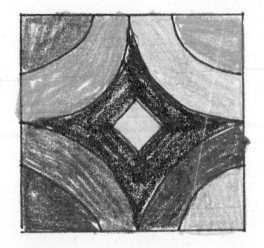

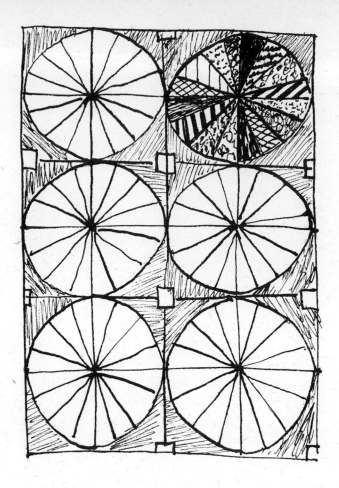

FIG. 75. *Early pinwheel designs for Spinning Wheel.*

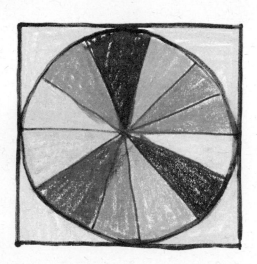

142

The pinwheel is constructed of pieced pie wedges of fabric that are then appliquéd to the block. The process is very like the Dresden Plate discussed earlier (see pages 105–112).

The usual way of handling pinwheels is by appliquéing them within blocks and piecing the blocks together. The Mountain Artisans designer had never been satisfied with the usual way. Her particular genius lay in treating the usuals (traditional) in unexpected ways. Instead of positioning the pinwheels within the blocks, she wanted to link the blocks and appliqué *over* them.

At first, she thought of blocks of a uniform size overlaid with circles of a uniform diameter, but that seemed monotonous. Next, she thought of varying the sizes of the blocks and covering seams with ribbon, and that was better (see fig. 76 page 143).

FIG. 76. *Preliminary Spinning Wheel design.*

For both circles and blocks, she wanted to use a brilliant spectrum of crisp solid reds, blues, yellows, greens, lavenders, and oranges. She did a plan of the pieced blocks indicating the ribbon borders and keying the colors by letter (see fig. 77 page 144).

To enable the women in the groups who would execute the piece to be certain of measurements and scale, she transcribed the design on graph paper (see fig. 78 page 145).

A close scrutiny revealed that there was still something amiss.

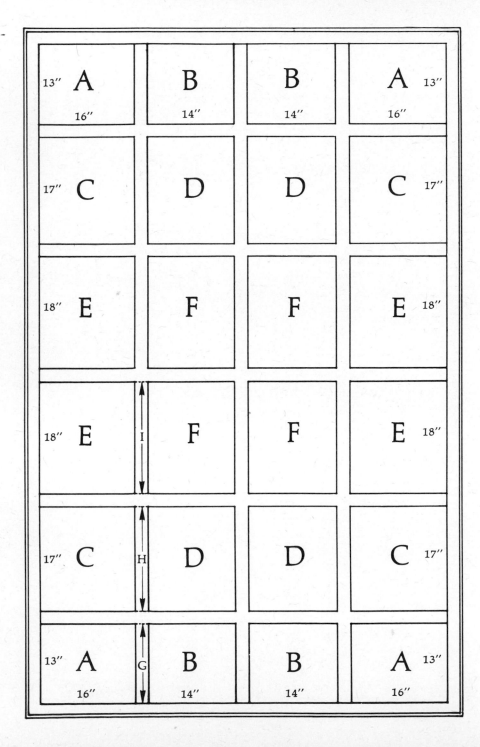

FIG. 77. *Plan of the pieced blocks for Spinning Wheel (each letter represents a color).*

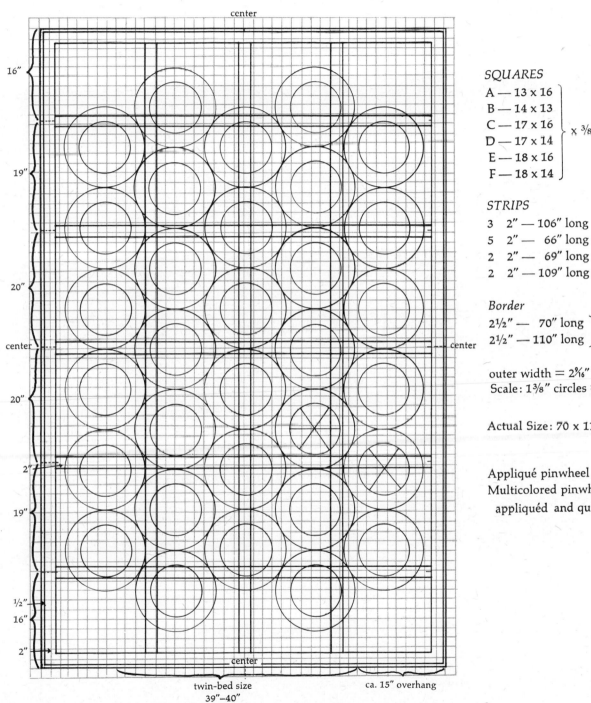

center

16"

19"

20"

center

20"

2"

19"

½"
16"

2"

center

twin-bed size
39"–40"

ca. 15" overhang

SQUARES
A — 13 x 16
B — 14 x 13
C — 17 x 16
D — 17 x 14
E — 18 x 16
F — 18 x 14
$\Big\}$ x ⅜" seam allowance

STRIPS
3 2" — 106" long
5 2" — 66" long
2 2" — 69" long
2 2" — 109" long

Border
2½" — 70" long
2½" — 110" long
$\Big\}$ + seam allowance

outer width = 2⁹⁄₁₆"
Scale: 1⅜" circles = 13⅞"

Actual Size: 70 x 110

Appliqué pinwheel
Multicolored pinwheels—pieced,
    appliquéd and quilted

FIG. 78. Graph paper
design of Spinning
Wheel.

145

What Dorothy really wanted was close to the feeling of a brilliant burst of fireworks. The uniform circles were too deliberate and geometric. They did not give her the sensation of the random razzle-dazzle of sky rockets and fiery pinwheels.

She jettisoned the uniform circles in favor of an array of circles in five different diameters. She did another color rendering, again keying the colors and fabrics by letter (see fig. 79 page 147). It looked very right.

Before the Spinning Wheel was completed, there would be alterations and shifts in placement. It was not until the quilting plot was rendered (see fig. 80 page 148) that all of the parts were in place to the designer's satisfaction. The marvelous thing about appliqué is that until the final sewing there is time for change and innovation.

The blocks of a traditional pieced quilt generally repeat each other and relate in a very specific way. Dorothy thought that there was no reason why the modern quilter had to be bound by this. A compositional relationship could as easily be built by balancing opposing geometric shapes—circles with squares, triangles with rectangles.

She began to doodle freely ranging over geometric forms (see fig. 81 page 149). The results were interesting. She did a more detailed drawing and called it Geometric #1 (see fig. 82 page 149).

In her sketch, she had indicated the use of patterned fabric, but the overall design was too strong. Patterns seemed to clutter it and destroy the purity of the forms. Strong, solid colors would do the reverse and enhance the design.

There was something else that was undeniable about Geometric #1. For all its geometric abstraction, there was an essentially thematic quality to it. It was intensely American in feeling and could only have been created in the heartland of this country by a native designer.

When it came to selecting colors, nationalism was the deciding factor, and Dorothy opted for red, white, and blue, using a strong pink as an accent (see Plate XII, facing page 134). Notice the manner in which the interesting quilting pattern echoes the geometric forms. In construction, the angular shapes were pieced, and the circles were appliquéd.

FIG. 79. Dorothy Weatherford's original color-keyed sketch for the Spinning Wheel quilt (see Plate XI between pages 62 and 63).

FIG. 80. *Quilting pattern for Spinning Wheel.*

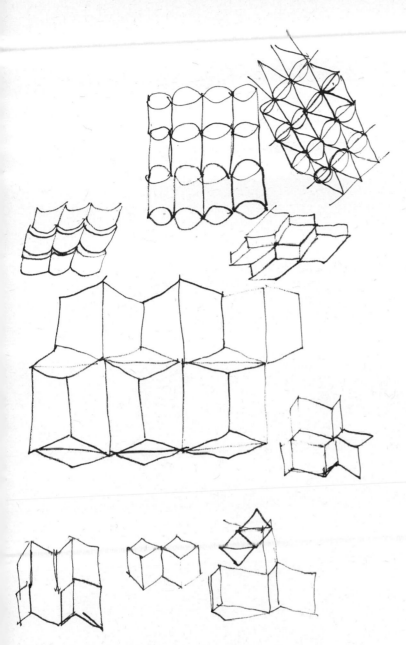

FIG. 81. *Geometric doodling.*

FIG. 82. *Geometric #1 (sketch).*

149

FIG. 83. *Sketches for geometric quilts.*

This is almost universally true of all quilting. Rounded or curved designs are appliquéd and straight lines are pieced. The obvious reason is that they are easier to cut and sew that way.

Once she had made a successful application of modern form to the old craft, Dorothy continued to explore geometric relationships and did a series of rough sketches for future quilts (see fig. 83 page 150).

Using the three basics of the old craft, there were endless possibilities for new avenues of design. Like a painting, a quilt is capable of conveying a multitude of expressions and styles. It is only a question of liberating one's approach to the materials and tools. The most avant garde painter uses traditional paint and canvas—but in a new way. The same can be true of the quilter.

New applications of traditional patterns, design experiments, a new revolution in the look of high fashion, tapestries of museum quality—there seemed to be no limit to the extent of Dorothy

150

PLATE XVI. *Contemporary Dorothy Weatherford gown with appliquéd skirt.*

PLATE XVII. *Contemporary Mountain Artisans' adaptation of traditional pieced quilt.*

PLATE XVIII. *Sharon Rockefeller in a pieced dress designed by Dorothy Weatherford.*

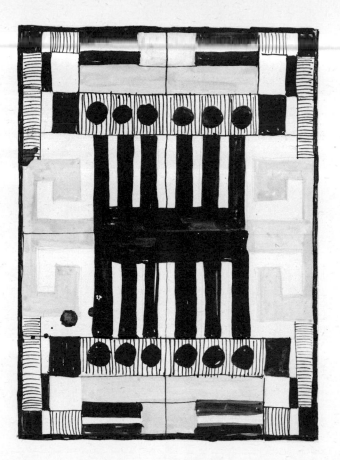

Weatherford's creativity within the craft framework. Following the paths she had opened can provide a wonderful adventure for both the old and new quilters.

The Weatherford results are so satisfying that the crafter may be encouraged to try some original experiments. That is the great gift that the Mountain Artisans has given to quilting. At the same time that they were preserving a venerable old craft, they were freeing it from slavery to tradition and revitalizing its application by means of new approaches to fabrics, designs, and purpose.

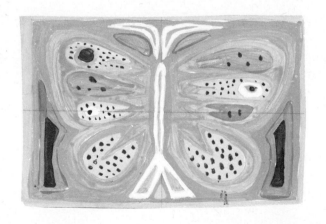

Block designs for the Rockefeller quilt.

152

CHAPTER SEVEN

"The committee decided unanimously to give a Special Award, which has sociological as well as fashion significance, to Mountain Artisans, organized by Sharon Rockefeller as a means of aiding a depressed area. Under the design direction of Dorothy Weatherford, the traditional crafts of patchwork and quilting have been revived. Modern and beautiful application of these skills in both home furnishings and fashion gave much-needed work to many women in Appalachia. It also helped spur the whole crafts movement."

> —TRUDY OWETT, CHAIRMAN OF 1972 COTY AMERICAN FASHION CRITICS' AWARDS

NEW YORK CITY is seldom visited by spring. Winter tumbles into summer without giving inhabitants time to store the furs of one season and bring forth the cottons of the next. But in 1970, spring dropped in on Beekman Place, a quaint little street that runs along the East River for two of the most elegant blocks in town.

The Mountain Artisans were at home to the press on their third New York trip. They were serving apple cider, sassafras tea, West Virginia ham, homemade breads, and a beautiful sunny line of Artisans creations. Sharon Rockefeller, Dorothy Weatherford, and Florette Angel, all attired in colorful samples from the collection, were among those acting as hostesses. The premises were courtesy of Sharon's in-laws, who resided in the exclusive building—a cooperative of a very different nature—and had persuaded their neighbors to allow the women to use one of the public rooms.

It was only one year since they had first ventured into the New York marketplace. Looking around the palatial surroundings, one could easily assume that the Mountain Artisans was the great Cinderella story of the year—even if the beautiful models did have to change behind up-ended ping-pong tables. All of the big names in the fashion world were in attendance. Magnificent garments not unlike the Floral Bouquet skirt (see Plate XIII facing page 134) drew applause from the knowing crowd.

When the Mountain Artisans' collection of big floral appliquéd skirts was first introduced (see Jungle Bouquet on page 70), it created a sensation. The women who bought these skirts have never regretted it, for they have not gone out of style and probably will not for years to come. With changes in the top (anything from a body stocking to chiffon and ruffles), they're as perfect for going to a ball as for an evening at home.

The Floral Bouquet skirt is as simple to make as the Jungle Bouquet skirt. Using an A-line skirt pattern, with no center seam, cut a skirt out in cotton of whatever color is to dominate the quilted skirt. In Plate XIII, it is black. Lay it front side down and cover it with a layer of dacron batting. Lay it aside. *Note:* In cutting, make certain that the skirt is exactly the desired length. There will be no hem. Follow the directions in figure 84, pages 156–157.

After the zigzag appliquéing is completed, attach the desired width of seam binding to the top and bottom. There is no hemming. The binding finished off the skirt. Complete the skirt according to the pattern instructions.

To make a Floral Bouquet quilt, construct in blocks of 18″ by 36″, otherwise, it will be difficult to turn the piece in the machine. Make as many blocks as are necessary to complete the quilt (See fig. 85 page 158.) The same rule of 1½ times as much fabric for flowers as area of the total applies. Sew the blocks together after completing the zigzag appliquéing. Instead of evening the blocks with fabric, overlap and underlap the flowers to cover the seams. Machine zigzag to finish them.

Assemble with backing and complete the cover with the desired width and color of seam binding on all sides.

For the Floral Bouquet quilt (shown together with the Animal Crazy quilt in Plate XV, facing page 135), black cotton backing and black velveteen binding were used.

For the Floral Bouquet quilt in Plate XIV, larger flower patterns were used in more delicate colors to achieve a boudoir effect. The same was true of the pink selected for backing and binding.

With success, the Mountain Artisans began to have such acute growing pains that they almost died of them. The first problem had been to grow large enough to play with the big kids, then the organization suddenly shot up. Overnight, it had reached a gangling adolescence, and the problem became a question of how to use these suddenly long limbs. They were so awkward, so difficult to manage. The original eight groups had become fourteen with the addition of the six from CBDP, which had come with the OEO grant. Sales had jumped to well over six figures. There was a desperate need for a central intelligence to coordinate the whole project, to pull together the sprawling body and make it function with grace and efficiency.

It was then that an energetic and enthusiastic young woman named Sally Wells appeared on the scene. Sally had a natural gift for management, a charming smile that masked an astute sense of business. Claudia Schechter has described her impact on the group. "Florette, Dorothy, Rita, and I were like random atoms bumping into things. The books showed total business failure, until her expertise started the chain reaction and harnessed our energy. Without her, there would be no Mountain Artisans."

Sally had a background that was diverse enough to cope with any situation. She had been acting director of the Peace Corps' project in Guatemala, where she had supervised a group of volunteers working with native handicrafts. Earlier, she had been in charge of the organization's speakers' bureau, juggling the schedules of countless lecturers all over the country.

She had spent ten years in New York City in a variety of jobs that ranged from managing "Video Vittles," a company that prepared the food used in television commercials, to putting together an audio-visual series, "French Civilization as Reflected in the Arts," to serving as business manager for a prominent designer.

Business management, the fashion world, idealism, a knowledge of handicrafts, and a sense of tradition—Sally could call upon something to handle almost every exigency that she might face as managing director of the Artisans.

Sharon Rockefeller encouraged her to apply for the job. The board approved her application, but, before she accepted the position

A

B

FIG. 84. *Construction of the Floral Bouquet skirt.*

    A. *Cut out three cardboard patterns and centers—10", 12", and 16". The centers are respectively 1½", 2", and 3".*

    B. *Using a great variety of fabrics (in all, totalling 1½ times as much as was necessary to cut out the skirt), outline and cut out the flowers and centers.*

    C. *Start overlapping flowers and centers on top of the batting and skirt backing. (For purposes of photography, only a block was used.) Securely pin in place, going through the layer of batting to the skirt body.*

    D. *For evening off the sides, top, and bottom, a piece of fabric can be cut and inserted under the flowers in any place that is not filled.*

C

D

E

E. *Pin in place and complete, covering the skirt.*

F. *Zigzag around the edges of the centers and flowers. Make certain to go through all the layers. To hold the flowers securely in place, set the machine's stitch-length regulator to just before the fine area. The stitch width should be approximately middle range. Be sure that the raw edges of the flowers and centers are right in the center of the zigzag stitch, or they will unravel.*

F

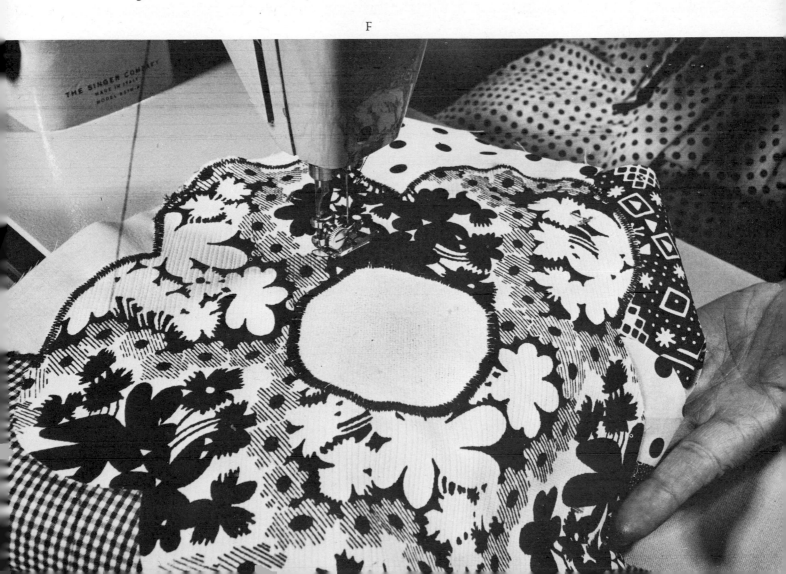

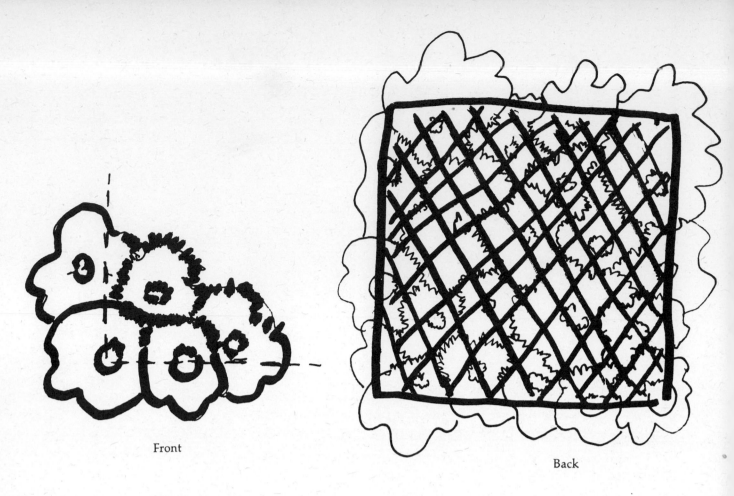

Front

Back

FIG. 85. *Floral Bouquet quilt block.*

Sally demanded and received the authority to reorganize the management and production, incorporating many new ideas of quality control.

Sally was the finishing detail in the managerial mosaic of Mountain Artisans. From VISTA, from the Department of Commerce, from Community Action, from the Appalachian Volunteers, from the Peace Corps—a disparate group of young women who had only their idealism in common had banded together to create a business that had higher goals than mere profit.

Purpose, pride, identity, and kinship are the pervasive feelings that one senses when visiting the rural sewing groups. One also senses them in the Charleston office. Beneath the efficient industry, the atmosphere of the quilting party is still very much alive. The

158

coffee pot is always on. When one of the sewing women drops by, there is time to stop, listen to complaints, gossip, and just plain visit for a spell.

Day-care centers are novelties in Charleston. For the Mountain Artisans staff, they're not necessary. As with the women in the hills, the child is always welcome. In Upsher County, Pearl Hornbeck and Velma Eckert work as a team. Their companion is the neighbor's child they look after every day. Pauline Bosley works busily at her machine to the accompanying clatter and chatter of nine children and one grandchild.

In Charleston, Rita Bank cannot find a babysitter for her infant, Jessica, and so Jessica is brought to work where a bed of fine quilts is made for her on the floor of Florette Angel's office. During school holidays, Dorothy Weatherford's three children wander in and out, building worlds of fancy amid bolts of brilliantly colored fabrics.

It is no wonder that the maternal feeling that inspired the Rockefeller quilt lingers in the workrooms of the Artisans, where a delightful array of children's coverlets is lovingly produced. Quilts like the Sam Henry (see fig. 91 page 165) can also be used as throws or wall hangings.

FIG. 86. *Block design for the Rockefeller quilt.*

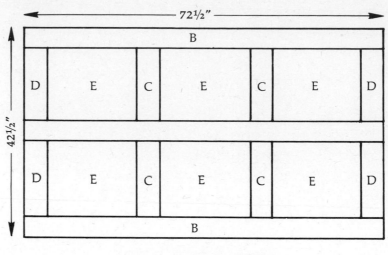

FIG. 87. *Sam Henry pattern.*

$$A = 72\frac{1}{2}'' \times 5\frac{1}{4}''$$
$$B = 72\frac{1}{2}'' \times 4\frac{7}{8}''$$
$$C = 15\frac{1}{4}'' \times 5\frac{3}{4}''$$
$$D = 15\frac{1}{4}'' \times 5\frac{3}{8}''$$
$$E = 15\frac{1}{2}'' \times 18\frac{1}{4}''$$

(All measurements include ⅜" seam allowance)

   The Sam Henry is so much fun and so easy to do that it can be made by any beginning quilter. Cut the parts necessary to assemble the Sam Henry quilt according to the plot given in figure 87. From a solid chintz of polished cotton, cut one panel *A*, 72½" by 5¼"; two panel *B*s, each 72½" by 4⅞"; four panel *C*s, each 15¼" by 5¾"; four panel *D*s, each 15¼" by 5⅜". From a lighter but complementary solid chintz or polished cotton, cut six blocks, measuring 15¼" by 18¼". All of these dimensions include ⅜" seam allowances on all sides. For each, a cardboard pattern can be made, if one does not want to keep measuring on the fabric. (See figs. 88 and 89 for instructions for making the animal patterns and directions for constructing the quilt.)

   When all the blocks and all the pieces are ready to be assembled, assemble them according to the plan shown in figure 87.

   Put in quilting frame along with batting and backing. Quilt

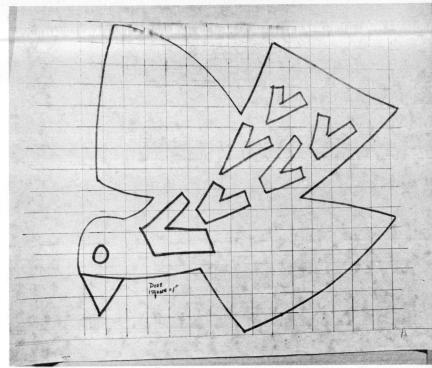

A. *Pattern for lion.*   B. *Pattern for dove.*

FIG. 88. *Making animal patterns for Sam Henry quilt. To make cardboard animal patterns for the blocks, rule off pieces of cardboard, the size of the blocks, into 1" squares and draw the animals to make certain that they will fit. Take into account the quilting borders and block seam allowances.*

C. *Pattern for turkey.*

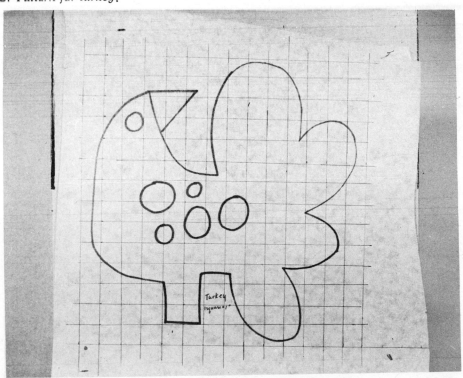

A

FIG. 89. *Construction of the Sam Henry quilt.*
    A. All the animal pattern pieces with the lion appliqué details.
    B. The kangaroo and its appliqué details.

B

C

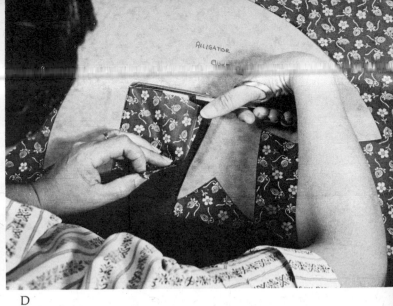

D

C. *Pin the pattern to the fabric it is to be made of.*

D. *Cut around the pattern.*

E. *Pin the animal body to the block (E of fig. 87).*

F. *Cut the appliqué pieces from a different but complementary fabric and pin them in place.*

G. *The block ready to be appliquéd. Zigzag the body and all the pieces to the block. Repeat this with each of the blocks. Use a different fabric for each animal body and for each set of appliqué details. It is possible to use the fabric of a body of one in the details of another.*

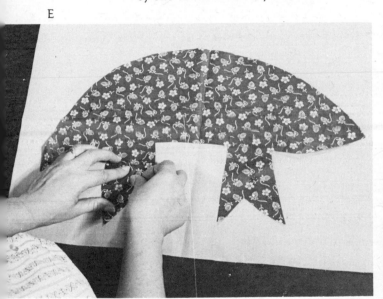

E

F

G

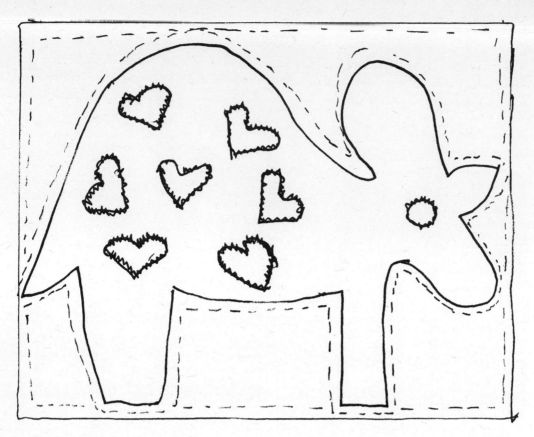

FIG. 90. *Quilting pattern for Sam Henry. Leaving a ½" margin around the animal, frame in quilting stitches. Leaving ½" within edge of panel, outline it in quilting. Treat all animal-pattern panels in the same manner.*

according to the plot in figure 90. Quilt around the animals, ½" from the appliqués. Bind in the same color as is used in panels *A, B, C,* and *D.*

Animal toys are another charming use for the animal patterns (see fig. 91 page 165).

Sunbonnet Sue is another of the Mountain Artisans' delightful nursery quilts (see fig. 92 page 169). It measures 32" by 42" and is made of crisp pastel solid and printed cottons. For this particular version, Dorothy Weatherford combined the traditional Sunbonnet Sue pattern, which came over from England with the colonists, and a series of charming nursery prints (see fig. 93 page 170).

A

FIG. 91. *Sam Henry animal toys.*

    A. *Sam Henry quilt and animals made from the appliqué patterns.*

    B. *Using the animal pattern, cut two bodies from the same fabric. One will serve as front and the other as back. If you are using a one-sided fabric, be sure to cut the animal with the right sides of the two pieces of fabric together.*

    C. *Cut, pin, and zigzag appliqué the details to the front half of the body.*

B

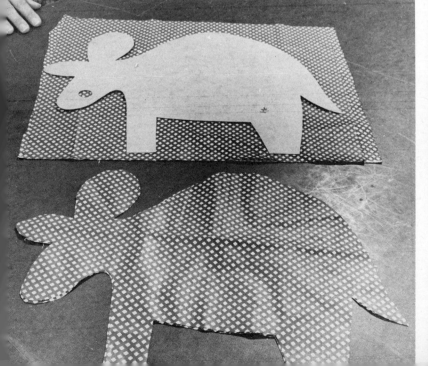

C

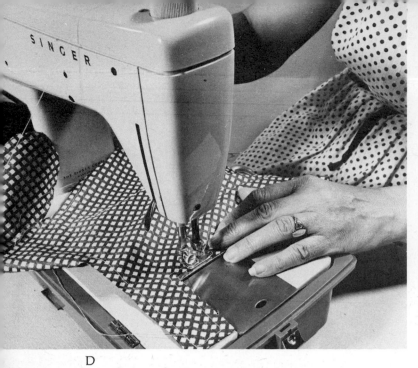

D

E

D. Sew the front and back of the animal together, with the reverse side of the fabric facing out. Leave a 3" opening on a straight side of the animal.

E. Make slits in all the corners, not quite up to the stitching, so the corners will turn neatly.

F. Through the opening, turn the animal front-sides out.

G. Use a pencil to make certain that all the details are reversed.

F

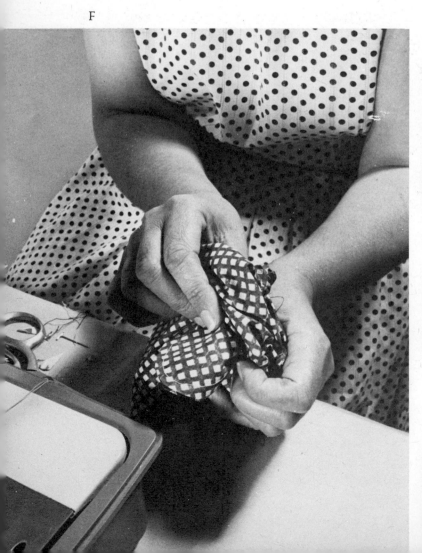

G

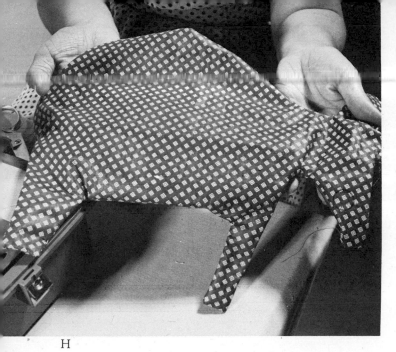

H

I

H. *The body ready for stuffing.*

 I. *Stuff through the opening.*

 J. *The animal stuffed. Make certain that there is stuffing in all of the limbs. Use dacron stuffing, so that the animal will be washable.*

K. *By hand, slip stitch the opening, completely closing it.*

J

K

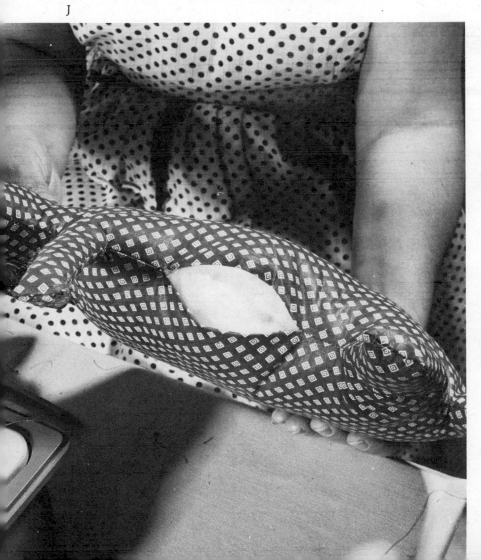

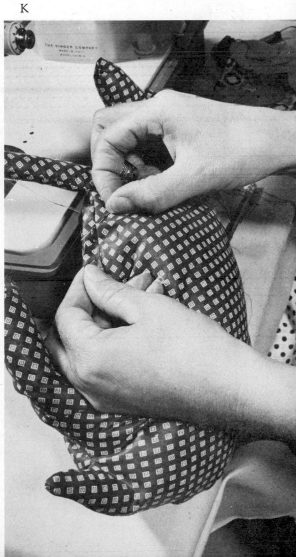

L. *The finished animal ready for cuddling.*

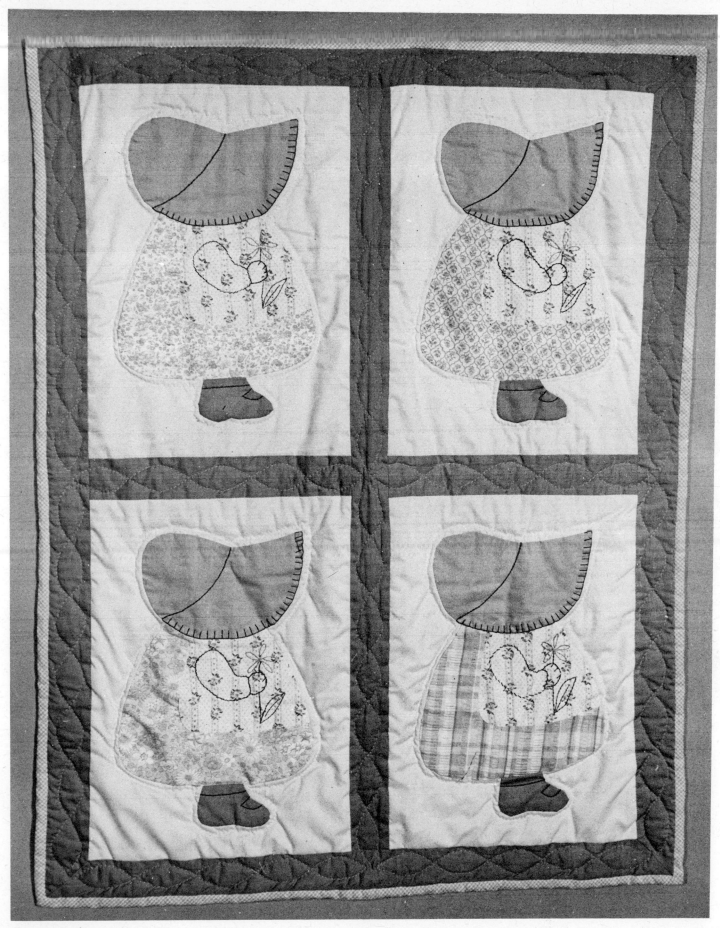

FIG. 92. *Sunbonnet Sue quilt.*

FIG. 93. *Nursery prints*.

To make the Sunbonnet Sue quilt, follow the directions given in figures 94–97. When the embroidering is completed, you are ready to assemble the blocks and pieces as indicated in figure 106. With batting and backing, place the quilt in the quilting frame or hoop and quilt according to the plan in figure 98. Quilt the pattern

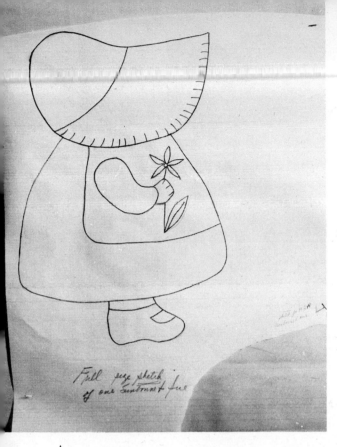

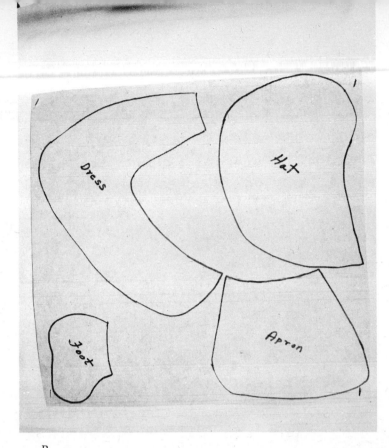

Full size sketch
of one sunbonnet sue

A

B

FIG. 94. *Pattern pieces for the Sunbonnet Sue figure .*

 A. *On ruled or graph paper, draw the figure to full scale. It should be 14½" high by 9½" wide.*

 B. *Cut out individual pieces of apron, hat, dress, and foot, and trace them on cardboard, adding a ⅜" seam allowance on all sides.*

in all the borders and ½" from the outline of the figure in the blocks. After quilting is completed, remove the quilt from the frame and bind the edges with color-keyed bias binding.

First there was the craft, and that was nearly as old as time. Then there were the women of the hills who had kept it alive for generations. And finally there was the idea of finding a way to have the women help themselves through a skill they practiced extraordinarily well.

The Mountain Artisans put it all together so well that, within four years of their founding, they had won a Coty Award—fashion's highest accolade, given by the American Fashion Critics—with crea-

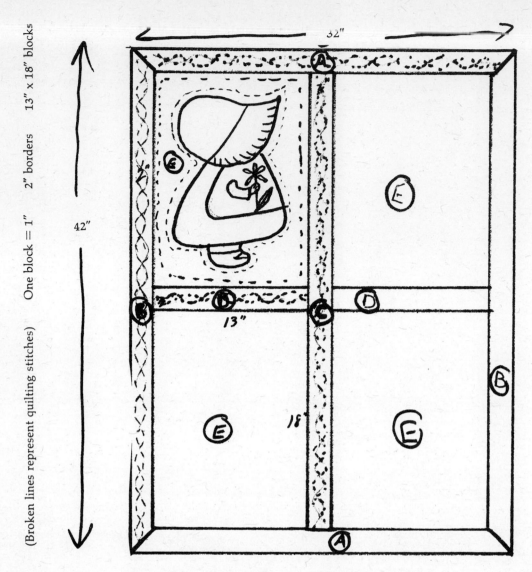

Fig. 95. *Scale drawing of Sunbonnet Sue quilt.*

Plan for assembling the quilt. Put aside the pattern pieces for the figure and cut the pieces for the rest. Cut the blocks (E) of a solid pastel, measuring 18¾" by 13¾". For the border pieces, use a complementary solid pastel. Cut two strips (A) measuring 2¾" by 32¾". Cut two strips (B) measuring 2¾" by 42¾". Cut one strip (C) measuring 2¾" by 38¾". Cut two strips (D) measuring 2¾" by 13¾".

172

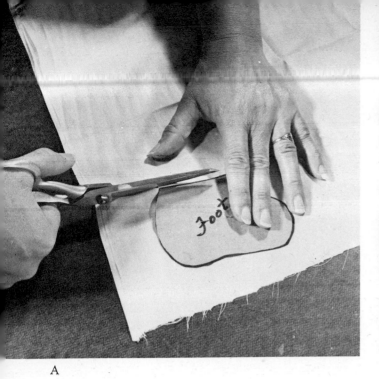

A

B

Fig. 96. *Construction of the Sunbonnet Sue quilt.*

 A. *From solid and printed cotton fabrics, cut four sets of the figure details, using the cardboard patterns as a guide.*

 B. *Lightly sketch the embroidery details in chalk and lay out and pin the figure pieces to the block (E) pieces. Tucking under the seam allowance, appliqué by hand.*

 C. *Buy some embroidery thread in a dark color. Each thread consists of six strands twisted together.*

 D. *Separate two strands and thread them through a needle.*

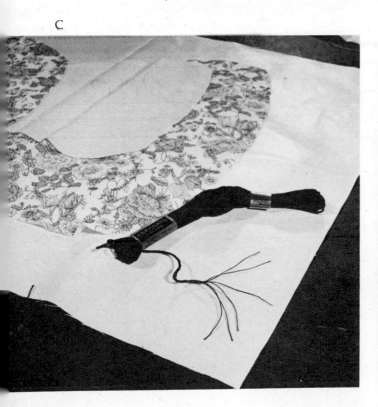

C

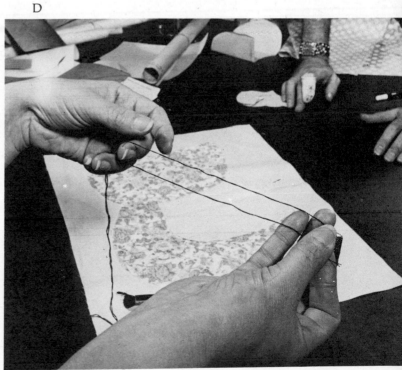

D

173

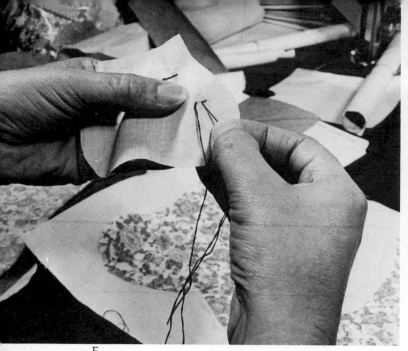

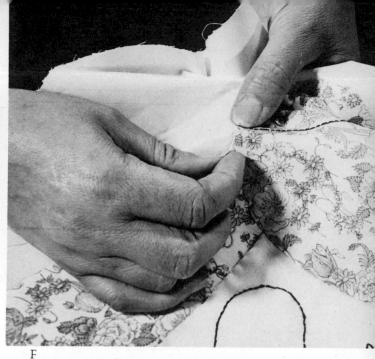

E

F

E. For most embroidery, a stem stitch is used. Start with a regular stitch. When the needle is brought back through the top of the fabric, it is inserted at the tail of the previous stitch. This doubling back is done for the entire line.

F. Embroider until all of the sketched detail on the appliquéd figure is filled.

FIG. 97. *Embroidering brim of the hat. For the brim, a buttonhole or blanket stitch is used.*

A. *About ¼" down from the top of the brim, bring the needle through from the back.*

B. *Insert the needle just above at the edge of the brim and bring it back out at its original point.*

A

B

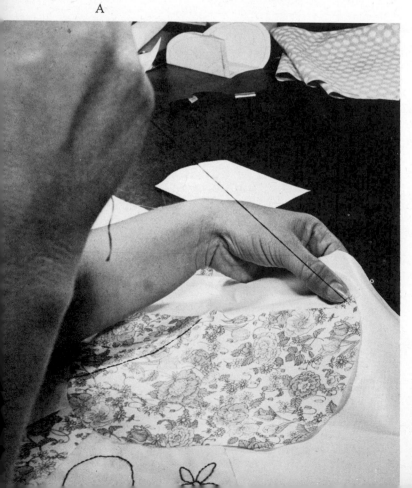

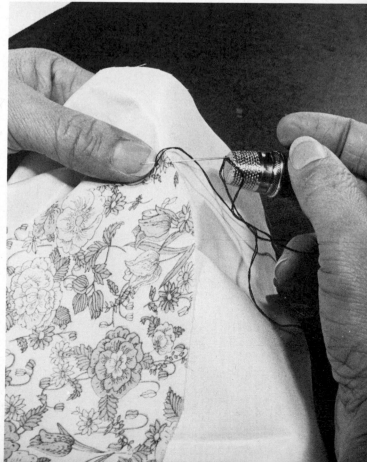

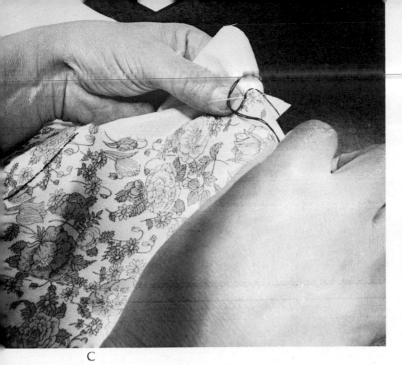

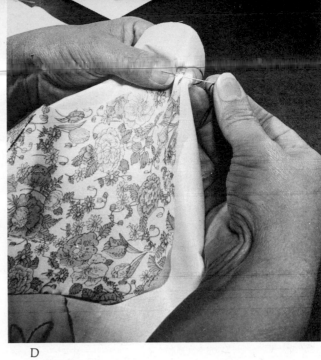

C

D

C. Loop the thread over the needle.
D. Pull the thread tight and start the second stitch.
E. Continue doing buttonhole stitches all around the edge of the brim.

E

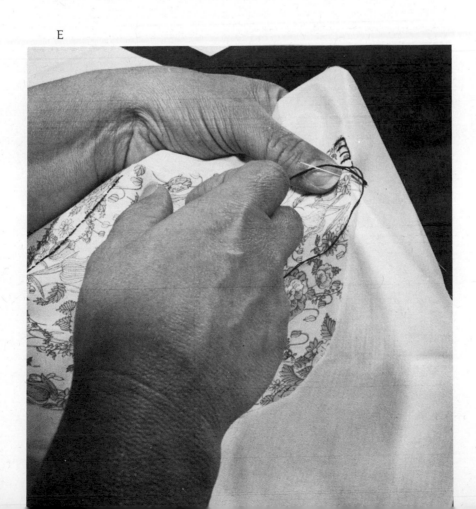

FIG. 98. *Quilting plan for Sunbonnet Sue.*

——————— = outline stitch embroidery

ⵌⵌⵌⵌⵌⵌⵌ = buttonhole or blanket stitch embroidery

- - - - - - - - - = quilting pattern

At a meeting in the Mountain Artisans' home office in Charleston, West Virginia. Left to right: Florette Angel, Sally Wells, Dorothy Weatherford, Rita Bank, Claudia Schechter.

176

tions like the one Sharon Rockefeller is shown wearing in Plate XVIII, facing page 151. It was bestowed by unanimous vote of the Awards Committee. It was the first time that a Coty citation mentioned the winner's work in home furnishings as well as in wearing apparel.

As the Coty Award remarked, the Artisans helped to spur the whole craft movement. Actually, what they have done is in the nature of a revival. It is part of a universal desire to return to a simpler way of life, to traditional American values that have become obscured in the jet stream of contemporary society. As a result, the old crafts have experienced a rebirth. In recent years we've seen vast numbers of people taking up needlepoint, macramé, rug hooking, and weaving. The Mountain Artisans has added quilting to the list.

This book is an invitation to their great American quilting party. Aside from the fun, there are the prettiest party favors—a bedspread, a skirt, a cover, a toy, a pillow, a wall hanging. So come on along. You'll be glad you did.

INDEX